W9-BAR-069

Raising
Pre-Teens

649.65
Dos

3/08

LaGrange Library
(845) 452-3141
www.laglib.org

DEMCO

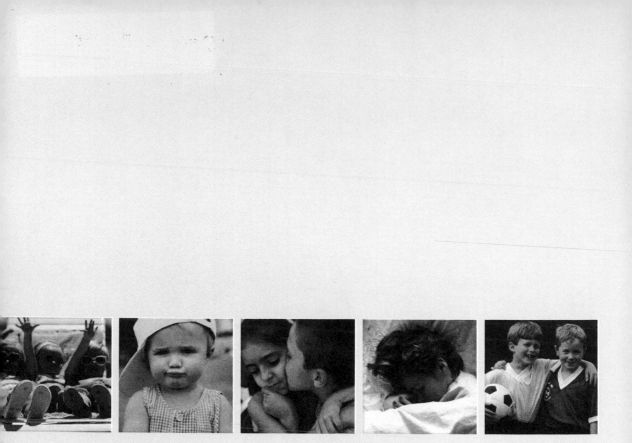

52 Brilliant Ideas

one good idea can change your life

~~LaGrange Library~~
~~(845) 452-3141~~
~~www.laglib.org~~

Raising Pre-Teens

Tips and Techniques for Making the
Most of Your Child's Terrible Tweens

Sabina Dosani, MD, and Peter Cross

A Perigee Book

A PERIGEE BOOK
Published by the Penguin Group
Penguin Group (USA) Inc.
375 Hudson Street, New York, New York 10014, USA
Penguin Group (Canada), 90 Eglinton Avenue East, Suite 700, Toronto, Ontario M4P 2Y3, Canada
(a division of Pearson Penguin Canada Inc.)
Penguin Books Ltd., 80 Strand, London WC2R 0RL, England
Penguin Group Ireland, 25 St. Stephen's Green, Dublin 2, Ireland (a division of Penguin Books Ltd.)
Penguin Group (Australia), 250 Camberwell Road, Camberwell, Victoria 3124, Australia
(a division of Pearson Australia Group Pty. Ltd.)
Penguin Books India Pvt. Ltd., 11 Community Centre, Panchsheel Park, New Delhi—110 017, India
Penguin Group (NZ), 67 Apollo Drive, Rosedale, North Shore 0745, Auckland, New Zealand
(a division of Pearson New Zealand Ltd.)
Penguin Books (South Africa) (Pty.) Ltd., 24 Sturdee Avenue, Rosebank, Johannesburg 2196,
South Africa

Penguin Books Ltd., Registered Offices: 80 Strand, London WC2R 0RL, England

While the author has made every effort to provide accurate telephone numbers and Internet addresses
at the time of publication, neither the publisher nor the author assumes any responsibility for errors,
or for changes that occur after publication. Further, the publisher does not have any control over and
does not assume any responsibility for author or third-party websites or their content.

RAISING PRE-TEENS

Copyright © 2004 by The Inifinite Ideas Company Limited
Cover art by Superstock
Cover design by Liz Sheehan
Text design by Baseline Arts Ltd., Oxford

All rights reserved.
No part of this book may be reproduced, scanned, or distributed in any printed or electronic form
without permission. Please do not participate in or encourage piracy of copyrighted materials in
violation of the author's rights. Purchase only authorized editions.
PERIGEE is a registered trademark of Penguin Group (USA) Inc.
The "P" design is a trademark belonging to Penguin Group (USA) Inc.

First American edition: September 2007
Originally published in Great Britain in 2004 by The Infinite Ideas Company Limited.

Perigee trade paperback ISBN: 978-0-399-53364-8

PRINTED IN THE UNITED STATES OF AMERICA

10 9 8 7 6 5 4 3 2 1

Most Perigee books are available at special quantity discounts for bulk purchases for sales
promotions, premiums, fund-raising, or educational use. Special books, or book excerpts, can also
be created to fit specific needs. For details, write: Special Markets, Penguin Group (USA) Inc., 375
Hudson Street, New York, New York 10014.

Brilliant ideas

Brilliant features

Each chapter of this book is designed to provide you with an inspirational idea that you can read quickly and put into practice right away.

Throughout you'll find four features that will help you to get right to the heart of the idea:

- *Try another idea* If this idea looks like a life-changer then there's no time to lose. *Try another idea* will point you straight to a related tip to expand and enhance the first.

- *Here's an idea for you* Give it a try—right here, right now—and get an idea of how well you're doing so far.

- *Defining ideas* Words of wisdom from masters and mistresses of the art, plus some interesting hangers-on.

- *How did it go?* If at first you do succeed, try to hide your amazement. If, on the other hand, you don't, this is where you'll find a Q and A that highlights common problems and how to get over them.

Introduction

Parenting pre-teens can be tough. Yet it's a task undertaken without formal qualifications. Family, friends, and well-wishers offer odd—sometimes very odd—advice, and then it's up to you. The only training is what you learn on the job. It's a steep learning curve and most novice parents learn quickly. But the parents who learn fastest are those who are able to benefit from others' experience, expertize, and brilliant ideas.

That's where this book and we come in. The 52 Brilliant Ideas format isn't our invention but it is ideally suited to our subject. It provides us with an opportunity to share hundreds of thoughts and practical suggestions to improve the quality of family life. A quick glance at the contents will give you something of the book's flavor. You'll find ideas devoted to reading, pets, cooking, and music. On a completely different tack there is another group of ideas about the maintenance of good behavior and boundary keeping. We haven't avoided the serious stuff, either. We deal with death and offer advice on how to salvage something from the wreckage if the bottom falls out of your marriage. Nor have we avoided other issues like sex, drugs, and cigarettes.

We decided against clustering topics together in neat chapters. Life isn't like that— neat and uncluttered—nor is parenthood. So you'll find *Wet, wet, wet* (dealing with bedwetting), followed by *Turn off the TV* (one of the few places where we're dogmatic), followed by our thoughts on finding and keeping quality child care.

As with other books in this series, most of the 52 ideas are connected to other topics that might provide relevant thoughts and suggestions. This demonstrates how our publishers and we feel these books are best used, as brain food for lateral thinkers. We'd be delighted to learn that parents have put our suggestions into practice. But these are only suggestions, launch pads for your own imagination, things to whet the appetite and get your creative juices flowing.

Many of the ideas we present may be familiar to you, others may be new variations on old themes, and hopefully there will be totally new ways of seeing and resolving old difficulties. We are students of the try-it-and-see school of parentcraft; if you haven't already signed up we suggest you do so. You just take in some interesting suggestions, see what works for you and your family, and throw out or modify everything that doesn't.

We'd like to thank the many parents and grandparents who have knowingly or otherwise contributed to this book with stories and ideas. Some of these stories didn't make it. One mother complained that her eleven-year-old hung around with her friends and made her wait ages after demanding a ride home. This went on for a while before she came up with her own solution: She arrived in her car in an old dressing-gown, wearing curlers. End of problem.

Then there are the little people who have provided so much vital information. Children, even small ones, will tell you things if you demonstrate that you are interested and prepared to listen. Parenting and family life is lived in public as well as in private at home. Good and bad examples are available for anyone who bothers to look.

The sorts of parents we feel will benefit from this book don't have bottomless pockets. And even if they did we'd advise against just buying a quiet life. One of the most important lessons any child needs to learn is that throwing money at life's difficulties is unlikely to provide long-term solutions. The best outcomes are more likely to come from imagination and planning. Most parents we know do not have unlimited time and energy to invest in the next generation. They live and function in the real world with real problems and difficulties, of which parenting pre-teens is only a part.

Parenting might, at times, be tough, but for the most part it can and should be fun, deeply rewarding, and life enhancing. Some parents thrive in this role while others struggle. Why this should be is something we have wrestled with in the process of writing this book. Then we saw something that illustrated this point perfectly. During a short train journey we noticed two mothers, each with two young children. Both moms struggled to get their strollers on board, but afterward everything was different. The first mother spent the journey shouting at her bored kids, who seemed intent on fighting each other and spoiling her cell phone calls. The other mother provided stimuli—early readers and unbreakable toys. The latter family talked together and the older child looked after his younger sister.

If these snapshots are typical of the rest of their lives, the quality of life in the two families couldn't have been more different. In one, boredom, misery, arguments, and public humiliation is the norm while for the other children train journeys were a stimulating experience with a relaxed and calm adult. The ability to put yourself in your children's shoes, seeing the world through his or her eyes, anticipating a range of problems, having responses ready for these and contingencies for the unexpected might not be the answer to all life's problems but, we suggest, it's a start.

1

It's my party

Hosting a successful party is something of a jewel in the parenting crown. Your mission, should you choose to accept it, is to plan the best party your pre-teen's friends have ever been to...without breaking the bank.

Birthdays, baptisms, bar mitzvahs. Their milestones becoming your millstone? Whether you're hosting a party that's big and noisy or small and intimate, our planning tips will help you steer smoothly through the pre-teen party circuit.

LOCATION, LOCATION, LOCATION

Hire a venue or party at home? Ultimately this comes down to two things: Your budget and how many fragile antiques you own. If you decide to hold the party elsewhere, like at the local swimming pool, be clear about what you're getting. Some places trick you with a low hiring fee, then force you to have their own poor-quality, but expensive, catering. If an entertainer is offered, check out how long for. An hour is often all you get, leaving you to amuse thirty children on unfamiliar turf.

Here's an idea for you... **Get one of your helpers to decorate children so that they are instantly part of the party theme. For instance, if you're having a pig party, give everyone a pin-on curly tail (easily made by twisting a pink pipe cleaner).**

HELP, I NEED SOMEBODY

The younger your kids are, the more help you'll need. Here's a quick way of working out how many extra pairs of hands to recruit:

- For under fives, one adult helper for every five children
- For six-year-olds, one adult helper for every six children
- For seven-year-olds, one adult helper for every seven children
- For eight-year-olds, one adult helper for every eight children
- For nine-year-olds, one adult helper for every nine children
- For ten-years-old and over, one adult helper for every ten children

TIME TO PARTY

For young children, shorter parties are certainly sweeter. We suggest most pre-teen parties should run from 3 to 6 p.m. Exceptions to this, like slumber parties, work better with slightly older, smaller groups. For a hassle-free party, plan every 30-minute slot and circulate a plan like this to helpers:

3:00 Play an icebreaker game
3:30 Time for a bouncy, lively game
4:00 Serve food and cake
4:30 Some quiet games while food goes down
5:00 Now some more boisterous games or competitions with prizes
5:30 Quieting-down game
6:00 Hometime

GENERATION GAP

Younger children happily play duck duck goose and musical chairs, but when pre-teens get to school age, parties become competitive. They can be quite snobby about your suggestions for games, pronouncing them "babyish." There's a lot of pressure on school-age children to have parties that are the hippest of the hip, so don't be too surprised if they suddenly won't be caught dead playing duck duck goose.

Kids bored of all the usual party games? Check out IDEA 15, _Generation games_.

Try another idea...

THE SECRET OF A SUCCESSFUL PARTY

The best parties are themed. The best theme is whatever your pre-teen is currently into. Themes can be anything from a favourite color to something more specific, like astronauts. Once you have a theme, carry it through, from the invitations to the goody bags, and the party will be a success. It doesn't matter what theme your child chooses, as long as it is reflected everywhere: decorations, costumes, games, music, and food. Involve your children in activities like making invitations as much as possible.

So if your child loves green, write invitations on green cards; decorate with green streamers and green balloons. Make it clear everyone has to wear green, even accompanying parents. Serve open cucumber sandwiches, celery with guacamole dips, olives, green peppers, green jelly, and other green snacks.

"The sooner every party breaks up, the better."
JANE AUSTEN, *Emma*

Defining idea...

Princess party

Little girls like to show off their ballet clothes. This is a great party to have outdoors, with a big bouncy castle. Star-shaped, glittery invitations set the tone well. Cardboard crowns can be improved by putting stickers on them.

Party like ancient Egyptians

Egyptian-themed parties work well with mixed ages and genders. Play pin the tail on the sphinx, hold a "walk like an Egyptian" competition, give one of your helpers an eye pencil and get her to draw Cleopatra-esque cat's eyes on girls. Or have an archaeological dig. In the week before the party, buy some cheap terra-cotta flowerpots. Paint each one a different color, then wrap in a towel and smash into four or five pieces with a hammer. Bury in a trough of sand. Divide the party guests into four teams; give each team a color. Each team has to dig in the trough, find pieces in their color, and stick them together with tape. To encourage the archaeologists, we suggest you bury some chocolate-covered coins, too.

Pirate party

Give pirates an eye patch (make these out of a circle of black felt and piece of elastic) or bandanna (washcloths are ideal). Treasure hunts make pirate parties special. You know better than us what sort of small gift your children's friends would like, so make that your treasure. You'll need to hide it well before the party and prepare clues. The first clue you write will lead them to the treasure. So if it's in the linen closet, write a clue like "The only closet upstairs that doesn't have mothballs in it." Hide that clue somewhere, say in the breadbox, and then write a clue leading children to the breadbox, working backward like this until you have around a dozen clues.

Wild parties

Safari sleepover parties are always a big hit with 7–9 year olds. These are evening parties, best held in warm weather. Make invitations on plain white cards, but get your pre-teen to decorate the back with zebra stripes for a striking look. The adult helpers (safari guides) help pre-teens cook their own barbecue supper before telling scary stories and camping outside in tents.

Glamour girls

Many eleven-year-old girls go through a very sophisticated stage. Want to give them a great party but your budget doesn't stretch to flying the whole class to Hollywood for makeovers and a shopping spree? Then have a *Breakfast at Tiffany's* party. Make invitations on Tiffany blue cards this time. Draw a circle in the corner and get your daughter to stick a big diamond-shaped sequin in the middle of it to look like a ring. Give them all a little lip gloss when they arrive. Nothing like a bit of gloss to add that touch of glam. For unusual place mats, laminate some photocopied pictures of Audrey Hepburn: feed the children croissants, bagels, pancakes, or a full cooked breakfast. Pick up some postcards of Audrey, put them in inexpensive frames, and use as prizes.

These are just a few suggestions. The best parties will be those themed around whatever your pre-teen is currently into. Mix and match themes if they seem too gender specific. Of course, "Pirates and Princesses" works better than "Safari Barbecue at Tiffany's."

THAT'S ALL FOLKS

When the party's over and parents come to collect their children, banish all thoughts of inviting them in. Letting a kid's party evolve into an adult one is a very bad idea. They rarely supervise their kids, who run riot in your home after all the helpers have given up and are helping themselves to your liquor cabinet.

Q My daughter wants a big expensive party and we just can't afford it. What do you suggest?

A   *Can you do a scaled-down version? Instead of flying sixty kids to Disneyland, could she take three close friends to the local theme park? If she won't budge, be up front about your budget. Could she have a big party as her main birthday present? Or pair up with a friend for a joint party that would halve your costs?*

Goin' potty

Potty-training marks the end of diapers and the beginning of underpants. End of babyhood, start of toddlerhood. Worried your youngster will never be continent and still need diapers in college?

Like many parents, you might be uncertain when to start potty-training. Most baby books suggest somewhere between 18 and 24 months.

The real answer: When your child is ready. This is usually nearer the 24-month mark for girls and up to 36 months for boys. Other children are fully trained at one year but this particular milestone is no indicator of a child's intelligence.

To find out if your child is ready or not, ask yourself the following questions:

- Is my child dry for at least two hours during the day?
- Does she clutch her diaper before wetting?
- Does he stop what he's doing for a few seconds before soiling?
- Can she follow simple instructions?
- Does he understand words like *potty*, *toilet*, and the words your family uses for bodily functions?

Here's an idea for you...

Once your child is 18 months old, keep a potty in the house. It might be too early to think about using it but talk about what it's for so it isn't a surprise later. Next time you change your child's diaper, talk about what he's done and explain that when he's older he'll use a potty.

- Can he pull down his diapers?
- Can she tell you when she needs to go to the bathroom?

If you can answer yes to most of these questions, your child is probably ready. If not, skip this idea. Starting too early delays learning later.

STEPS FOR SUCCESS

The secret of successful potty-training is to have a routine that everyone, including grandparents, child-care providers, and babysitters, adheres to. Many parents find it easier to potty-train in the summer. Children need to be able to remove clothing and in warmer weather they wear less and usually manage better. Summer clothes tend to be easier to wash, so accidents aren't as upsetting. Encourage toddlers to tell you when they have wet or soiled their diaper. The feeling of "needing to go" develops after realizing that they have been. Teach them how to pull down their pants and to ask for the potty.

Next, get them to tell you when they need to go and make sure a potty is handy. Look for clues—a stop in activity, squatting, or a screwed-up red face—and prompt them "Do you need to use the potty?" As well as providing the potty when it is clearly needed, sit your child on the potty as part of the morning routine prior to getting dressed and at bedtime, and also twenty minutes after meals.

Many children manage to use the potty during the daytime but wet the bed. Occasional bedwetting is normal up to the age of seven, but if frequent nighttime wetting is getting you and your child down, look at IDEA 5, *Wet, wet, wet.*

Try another idea...

This is exploiting basic physiology: Twenty minutes after eating, many toddlers need a bowel movement. Children learn to associate urinating voluntarily with sitting on the potty if they sit on it regularly at times they would normally go. Don't force a child to sit on a potty and if he doesn't go after a few minutes, take him off. Children associating potties with boredom or coercion are less likely to use them. Be patient. Some children learn in a couple of weeks, but they are unusual. It can take up to six months and boys usually take longer than girls.

"You can lead a child to the potty but you can't make him go."
DR. DANIEL KESSLER, pediatrician and potty-training expert

Defining idea...

Defining
idea...

"Modern parents believe toilet training should be an easy and casual affair. It used to be thought that children should act like 'little adults.' Like many things that used to be thought, this is true. In fact, now more than ever. Today's real adults are self-involved, impulsive, inarticulate, and spend as much time as possible out playing. They can't sit still, don't like to get dressed up, and hate every kind of activity that requires self-restraint. Adults are the children of today, and therefore children have to be adults because there's only so much room in the world for kids."

P. J. O'ROURKE

It doesn't matter if you decide to use a potty or a modified toilet seat, but if you do opt for a seat, provide a step up. If you use a potty, pick a color your child likes. Some toddlers are frightened they will be flushed down the toilet. You can minimize this by making a game of waving "bye-bye" after flushing. Explain that people don't go down the toilet. If they don't understand, play with a doll's house toilet and little doll's house people and get them to see if they can get the people down the toilet. If the potty is in the bathroom, extend the light pull, if you have one, so toddlers can turn the light on easily. Praise all attempts at using the potty. Accept that accidents happen. Don't punish or criticize. Once your toddler is a successful potty user, go on a special shopping trip and let her choose some "grown-up" underwear.

Q   Why does our son only use the potty for his mother and not for me?

A   *This often happens when one parent has been more involved in potty-training, but it is easily corrected. Mom should slowly retreat from potty time. Initially, both of you should go with your son to use the potty. After a few days, Mom could wait outside the bathroom door and after a few days of that, Dad could take him on his own. If parents are separated, it can help if your son uses the same potty at both households and if both parents use the same routine.*

Q   My daughter was potty-trained but she seemed to forget how to use it when her brother was born and is back in diapers after frequent accidents.

A   *Don't panic. Children who feel stressed by a big change like a new brother or moving often slip back a little. Take the pressure off. Spend some time on your own with her, doing both fun and mundane things so she doesn't feel excluded. Let her stay in diapers for a few weeks and then try again when she feels more secure.*

How did
it go?

11

3

Squabbling siblings

You're about to put your feet up with a well-deserved glass of Chardonnay when shrieks are heard from the bedroom above. The kids are fighting again. Can't they give you a moment's peace? We think so. Here's how.

It might not feel like it at the time, but sibling squabbles are part of life's rich tapestry. How brothers and sisters get along together matters, as it molds the sort of adults we become. Learning to resolve arguments teaches children how to take turns and ways of getting along with others.

Successfully negotiating these conflicts teaches patience, tolerance, managing setbacks, and agreeing to differ without losing face. You can reduce tension and stress by providing your children with social skills useful in school and with friends.

Here's an idea for you... **Get 'em early. Teach young children to stop, listen, think, and choose when they get into an argument. *Stop* what they are doing, take turns to *listen* to each other, *think* of lots of ways to solve the conflict, and *choose* ways that they can both live with. Next time you see or anticipate a squabble or fight brewing, use it as a learning opportunity. Comments like "It's OK to be angry with your brother for tearing a page out of your book, but in this family we don't hit people with the shovel" are helpful. If you feel pressured to take sides, tell them you know they can sort it out themselves but you'd like to hear how they handled it. When children get upset or angry, help them find ways to express feelings: squeezing salt dough (see IDEA 46, *Save it for a rainy day*), scribbling on an old newspaper with a red crayon then scrunching it up, hitting a pillow, playing noisy games with foot stamping or loud clapping. Suggest older children write angry statements in a diary.**

SPACE INVADERS

Ensure your kids have their own space to store toys and books. "Please knock" signs on bedroom doors reinforce a sense of ownership. Children sharing rooms need exclusive shelf space, part of a closet, or drawstring toy bags. Our friends have divided their children's bedroom using different colored rugs and masking tape for each child. All the children's shared possessions are stored in communal areas like the kitchen and living room, but individual's toys are kept in that child's space, and siblings must ask each other's permission to play with them.

STAY OUT OF IT

Sibling squabbles are children's business, and you should only get involved when someone is about to be hurt. Avoid taking sides or trying to sort it out. Mostly you won't have been there at the onset so won't have the full picture. The son who you think started it may have been provoked by his sister. Once children realize you remain neutral, fighting tends to dissipate. Set up a squabble corner and impose a family rule that children can only argue if they go to the squabble corner.

Children often argue because it gets parental attention. Donna might pick fights for this reason, and when Mom or Dad rescues Alison, Alison feels bad and picks a new fight at the next opportunity. Far better to give both girls attention for good behavior. Catch them when they are not fighting and let them know you've noticed. Say things like: "The way you shared the paints with Alison was great" and "You two played well all afternoon and I'm pleased" demonstrate that your kids don't need to fight to get your attention. If you find it hard to ignore arguments, retreat elsewhere in the home and play some music to drown out the shouting.

ALL THE WORLD'S A STAGE

Show children constructive ways to resolve conflicts. If you plan to get a refund for a broken toaster, take them with you. Explain what will happen. If they see you sorting out a problem assertively, they learn an important skill. If they see you arguing with your partner, make sure they see you making up.

Try another idea...

Children need to know what is expected. If you want them to put dirty clothes in the laundry basket before bedtime, say so. Rules need to be the same every day as inconsistency is confusing and may cause children to act up. There's more about how to involve children in setting rules and how to enforce them in IDEA 37, *Not in our house.*

Defining idea...

"Siblings are important because you know them the longest. You will probably outlive your parents and you don't meet your friends or your husband until later, but your sisters are there for almost the same time that you are."
ERIKA DUNCAN, feminist and novelist

STOP COMPARING

"Your sister does the dishes, but you never do."
"Why can't you practice playing the triangle like your brother?"

Comparing siblings sets them up against each other. Concentrate instead on getting them to work together. Give them team tasks like putting away all their toys in half an hour, rather than seeing who can tidy their room first.

"Comparison is a death knell to sibling harmony."
ELIZABETH FISHEL, educator and journalist

"There are only two things a child will share willingly: communicable diseases and its mother's age."
DR. BENJAMIN SPOCK, pediatrician and child-rearing guru

Q   **I can't help getting involved because my children hit each other. I couldn't possibly leave them alone in case they hurt each other.**

How did it go?

A   *We agree you need a zero tolerance violence policy. Parents should agree on sanctions for violent behavior and children need to know them. Have a look at Idea 18, Nursery crimes, for more on enforcing sanctions. Generally, if children are fighting and you are worried one will get hurt, intervene calmly and quickly separate them, then step back. Don't shout or be drawn into the dispute. Intervene because a rule has been broken, not to take sides or to sort it out.*

Q   **I find it hard to treat both children equally because they are so different and I think they pick up on this.**

A   *Don't worry. It's impossible to treat children equally. They need different privileges and responsibilities depending on their ages, genders, and personalities. The trick is to treat each one individually and spend designated time with both. Every child has unusual quirks and interests. Focus on these, making each child feel unique.*

4

Off duty

Who's babysitting for tonight's party? Leaving your children with a teenager who wants your home to herself? Can't drink because you're driving her home? Costs more than the night out? You have two options: stay in forever or read this chapter.

If you are able to root out a supply of babysitters, great. A few parents we know have used successive members of the same family and forged a close relationship between the two families.

Sadly, this is rare. For most parents it's a choice between arranging babysitting swaps with friends, meaning you can never go out with them, or trusting a teenager and never really relaxing on nights out.

(TROUBLE)SHOOTING TEENAGE BABYSITTERS

You already know why teenagers babysit. To play house and be paid for it. Luckily, some of them have basic childcare skills. Others don't know where to start. Help them by introducing them to the children, explaining the usual bedtime routine, leaving a list of contact numbers, and sticking to the time you say you'll be back. You

Here's an
idea for
you...

Instead of wasting hours calling around the babysitting circle and leaving messages, set up an email list or encourage members to email their availability and requests every week.

could also suggest some calming games (take a look at Idea 1, *It's my party*) in case your kids get up and are excitable. Remember, you are employing the babysitter, so encourage mature behavior by drawing up a contract stipulating rules about using your phone, entertaining boyfriends or girlfriends, children's bedtimes, and the hourly rate. Babysitting doesn't have to cost more than the rent. Try bartering with your babysitter: she babysits, you give her a driving lesson.

GOING AROUND IN CIRCLES

A babysitting circle is a cashless scheme, where tokens are swapped for sitting time and other parents look after your children. That's right: free babysitting by experienced parents.

To set up a circle, you'll need a group of at least four local families. Bear in mind that if you only choose people you like, it limits who you can spend your nights out with, as your friends will be babysitting. Get some plastic money (impossible to photocopy), give everybody a dozen coins, and you're ready to party. Want to go out this weekend? Phone around the circle and see who can sit. Circles needn't be evening only. You can drag your pre-teens to the store, hairdresser, or dentist, but why bother?

We suggest swapping one token for every hour before midnight, double tokens after. Some circles have more sophisticated arrangements whereby an additional tariff is charged for premium evenings like New Year's Eve. Strict circles impose fines, like one voucher for every twenty minutes a couple is late coming home.

Babysitting circles are only sustainable if everyone plays fair, putting in as many tokens as they take out. Once people start to feel exploited—for example, if people offer money instead of tokens—the scheme is doomed. The best circles we know are made up of like-minded parents who become friends and a social network that supplements the circle's core purpose.

Used up all your tokens? Phone around the babysitting circle and offer to do housework, ironing—in fact, anything legal—and like Cinderella, you shall go to the ball.

A GRAND IDEA

If grandparents live locally, it's understandable to look to them for babysitting, but eventually they, too, become resentful. If your parents are willing sitters, why not get them involved in your babysitting circle? While they're unlikely to need tokens for childcare, they could exchange them for services like home repair, gardening, or ironing. Once the offer's in place, you'll find most grandparents' priority is time with your pre-teens, rather than turning a profit.

"The care of children is infinitely better left to the best-trained practitioners of both sexes who have chosen it as a vocation, rather than a harried and all too frequently unhappy person with little time or taste for the work of educating minds."
KATE MILLETT, feminist author of the bestselling *Sexual Politics*

"Children have a massive impact on your relationship. If you don't have time for each other as a couple, or are only fit to crash out in front of the TV every evening, you can start to feel rejected and resentful. You need time together, away from the house. A night out and a bottle of wine can make you feel needed and loved again."
DENISE KNOWLES, mother of three and relationship counselor, family therapist, and advice columnist

21

WHEN IT'S YOUR TURN TO SIT IT OUT

We babysat for work colleagues and arrived when the younger children were already in bed. When three-year-old Kate woke up crying, she wanted Mommy and was horrified to find herself with two four-eyed strangers. She settled down eventually but we resolved always to meet children before they go to bed. We don't need to tell you to check that you have a contact number for parents.

How did it go?

Q **We've used the same babysitter for over a year. Last Saturday we came home and found her drunk—her first boyfriend just dumped her. Should we consider this a one-off and use her again or give her the boot?**

A *Show her the door. Thank her for her past services and look for someone else. Your pre-teens' welfare is more important than her feelings.*

Q **Even if we only have a meal locally, one of us can't have a drink and we have to leave early as our babysitter has to be driven home. Any suggestions?**

A *The cheap option: Let your babysitter sleep over and drive her home the following morning. The expensive option: Pay for her to get a cab home.*

Q **Our fledgling babysitting circle is just not taking off: nobody wants to go out and waste tokens. Help!**

A *When tokens are scarce, everyone hoards them. Why not give everyone six extra tokens, or provide incentives for grandparents to join your circle (see Idea 12, Grandparents: help or hindrance?).*

5

Wet, wet, wet

Enuresis is a cruel and humiliating condition. Hard on pre-teens, parents, and your washing machine. Stop just dreaming about dry nights...here's how to make them happen.

Experts divide bedwetting (or enuresis, as it's known in the trade) into two types:

- *Primary nocturnal enuresis* is the name we give to bedwetting in children who have never been dry at night.
- *Secondary nocturnal enuresis* refers to bedwetting in children who have had dry nights for at least six months in the past.

We only consider bedwetting to be a problem in kids who are five or older, because before then they're not able to control bladder muscles.

Bedwetting can be a dreadful stigma for those children affected by it. Sometimes siblings pick up on it and can be unmerciful in their assault on a brother or sister. The sense of shame can induce unbearable anxiety before sleepovers and fear that the rest of the school, Cub pack, or Brownies will know their guilty secret. Many more boys than girls wet the bed. You may have noticed it runs in families and will be relieved to hear most pre-teens have stopped bedwetting by the time they reach puberty.

Here's an idea for you...

Next time your pre-teen wets the bed, why not get him involved in washing the soiled sheets? This isn't intended to be punitive. On the contrary, children feel part of the solution, not just a pain. They learn useful domestic skills in the process. In our experience, pre-teens prefer to be involved in the cleanup rather than guiltily watching you having to do it for them.

Defining idea...

"Soon after I arrived at St. Cyprian's I began wetting my bed. I was aged eight, so this was a reversion to a habit which I must have grown out of at least four years earlier. Nowadays I believe bedwetting in such circumstances is taken for granted. It is a normal reaction in children who have been removed from their homes to a strange place. In those days, however, it was looked on as a disgusting crime for which the proper cure was a beating."
GEORGE ORWELL

"Will he ever grow out of it?" you wonder. We know you've probably tried all the sensible things, like limiting drinks before bedtime, sending your pre-teen to the toilet before going to bed, and praising him for dry nights, but what if none of these makes any difference?

WHAT A STAR

Star charts work well with younger pre-teens. For every dry night, your child gets a star. You'll need a calendar with enough space to stick or draw a star under each day. We've found it works best if the calendar is used only for this purpose, rather than for other family business. Some children like to keep them by the bed. Every ten stars can be "cashed in" for a treat (see Idea 17, *Treats*). Having something to work toward can be a powerful motivator.

ALARM

Bedwetting alarms teach your pre-teen to get up and use the toilet rather than wetting the bed. Kids wear these devices under pajamas or a T-shirt. Two moisture sensors complete an electrical circuit that sounds an alarm as soon as they come into contact with urine. When the alarm sounds, the idea is that kids get up, go to the bathroom, and change into dry clothes if necessary. You can help him by providing a flashlight or bedside lamp so he can get to the bathroom easily in the middle of the night. Perseverance is key. It takes up to twelve weeks for pre-teens to learn when their bladder is full and to get up to use the toilet.

OVER-LEARNING

So your pre-teen's used an alarm successfully and wakes up to go to the bathroom. Great, but if she stops using the alarm right away, the wet beds will be back. She needs to do something called "over-learning." All this means is that she needs to drink a couple of glasses of water before going to bed, so she learns to stay dry even when she goes to bed with a full bladder. Mastered this? Good. Stop using the alarm on Wednesdays and Saturdays. After a couple of dry weeks, only use the alarm every other night and then only twice a week for at least another four weeks.

MEDS FOR DRY BEDS

Children who bed-wet feel bad about themselves. It has a detrimental effect on their confidence and many underperform at school or find it harder to make friends. Check out IDEA 35, *Highflyers*.

Try another idea…

"While you yourself may be discouraged because of the never-ending laundry, remember that your child is not intentionally or deliberately trying to make life difficult for you. The object is to remove the sense of guilt and shame he might have about bedwetting and, instead, promote a feeling of optimism about his eventual ability to control his bedwetting."
Dr. CAROLYN WEBSTER-STRATTON, child psychologist and parenting expert

Defining idea…

We all produce a hormone called anti-diuretic hormone (ADH), also known as vasopressin. Its job is to concentrate urine, which stops our bladders from overfilling. A synthetic copy of ADH is available as a nasal spray and is sometimes prescribed to slow pre-teen's urine production.

How did it go?

Q **Our four-year-old son wets the bed about once a month. It's very distressing for him. What can we do?**

A *It sounds as if he's too young to control his bladder all the time. The occasional accident is common at his age. He'll probably grow out of it. Once he sees you're not too worried, he'll be less distressed.*

Q **My husband wet the bed and now our son does. Has he passed it on?**

A *About three-quarters of bedwetting children have parents who used to wet the bed. Your pre-teen will probably become dry at night at the same time as his dad did.*

Q **Why is it that my eight-year-old doesn't wet the bed at friends' homes, but does it here? Is she doing it on purpose?**

A *No, she isn't bedwetting at home on purpose, but it must be difficult not to think so when she seems to be able to stay dry when it's important to her. We suspect that when she goes to her friends, she is so worried about wetting, that she doesn't sleep as deeply as she does at home. If she's anxious and sleeps badly, she is less likely to have accidents. Try an enuresis alarm.*

6

Turn off the TV

Want your children to be healthier, happier, and have a greater sense of purpose? Had enough of them pestering "Buy me one of those," only to be bored and discard their new toys after five minutes? It's easy. Just press a button.

What is the greatest gift you could give your children? We asked lots of parents, and the winning answer won't surprise you. Time. Time has become a luxury.

There just don't seem to be enough hours in the day for children to do their homework, go to after-school clubs, learn to play piano, go to sports practice, go to ballet, go to Cub Scouts, play with friends, have conversations, have family mealtimes, hear bedtime stories, or put on a family play. TV has elbowed in and taken over, robbing children of an estimated four hours a day. This adds up to 14,560 hours or one year and eight months spent in front of an electrical appliance over ten years. If you don't believe us, why not do your own time and motion study of your pre-teens' TV habits? If you want to give them up to two years extra childhood, it's time to trash the television.

Watching TV is bad for children's physical and mental health. Toddler TV addicts learn to speak around a year later than their unaddicted friends. Older pre-teens

Here's an idea for you... **Turn off the TV for a week. Remove the plug and declare it "broken" if you're worried about family resistance. If you have TVs in every bedroom and the kitchen you'll have to come up with something more creative. At your next family meeting, ask everyone what they really missed watching. Most families who do this experiment like having their free time back so much, they decide to trash the TV. If you don't want to go it alone, look out for International TV Turn-Off Week, which takes place every April.**

Defining idea... *"Research has shown primarily negative health effects on violence and aggressive behavior, sexuality, academic performance, self-image, nutrition, dieting and obesity, substance use, and abuse patterns."* AMERICAN ACADEMY OF PEDIATRICS on children and television

who watch more than two hours a day have decreased attention spans, poorer memory and recall, and are more likely to make mountains out of molehills as they are so used to being drip-fed drama. Lethargy, sluggishness, and decreased creativity are hallmarks of children who spend their lives staring at a piece of furniture when they are not in school or sleeping.

BUT IT'S EDUCATIONAL

If this was true, children who watched the most TV would get the highest marks and best school reports. TV transmits opinions. Education gives children the skills to acquire, make sense of, and use information from different sources. Instead of TV, we suggest farms, art galleries, museums, zoos, drama workshops, and unstructured free time for imaginative play. You may resolve only to watch good educational programs. But for how long? It won't be long before you and the rest of the household are passively gawking at the garbage that surrounds the good stuff and you're back on a diet of junk TV like everyone else. Watching films in the theater or on DVD has much more in common with reading books, allowing you and your children to consolidate the experience.

Defining idea...

"*Television: a medium. So called because it is neither rare nor well done.*"
ERNIE KOVACS, comedian

Defining idea...

"*By the age of eighteen, the average child has witnessed 200,000 acts of violence, including 18,000 simulated murders, on TV. It is not always easy to provide clear, consistent structure for children, but providing it often helps keep children safe and helps them grow to be responsible adults.*"
JEAN ILSLEY CLARKE, parenting expert

Given the box the boot? And your kids are wondering what to do with four extra hours a day? Check out IDEA 52, *Something for the weekend*, or IDEA 46, *Save it for a rainy day*.

Try another idea...

"*Most parents say 'sometimes I just need some time to myself and I put the kids in front of the TV for a bit.' They think TV is helping them deal with the demands of parenting. But just the opposite is true. TV is designed to wind kids up. Frantic cartoons, screaming presenters, and loud, multicolored commercials go streaming into your child's eyes and ears. They come out again with a bang, at mealtime or bedtime. TV spoon-feeds children a steady dose of rapid-fire, happy noises, so they never learn to create their own good times.*"
DAVID BURKE and JEAN LOTUS, *Get a Life!*, produced by the White Dot anti-TV campaign

Defining idea...

29

How did it go?

Q **I'm convinced and we no longer have a TV, but whenever I take my children to play with their cousins, my sister always has the TV on in the background and it's really annoying. What can I do?**

A *Try being direct and say something like "We've come to visit you, not the TV. Could you please turn it off?" If that doesn't work, save your juicy gossip until her favorite program is on, then talk right through it. Alternatively, plan meetings around an activity and meet at the swimming pool or ice rink instead.*

Q **I got rid of the TV and the children are bored stiff. Help!**

A *Fantastic. Boredom is really important. It motivates children to do or create something that will make them happy. Because your children have been used to watching TV, boredom is probably a new feeling and they might be a bit frightened of it. In our experience, children without TV don't stay bored for long. Given appropriate creative outlets, freedom, and responsibility, they find their own answers to "What can I do next?" In a few weeks they'll be more inquisitive and inventive than ever.*

Q **We've sold the TV, but our children are furious. They're saving their pocket money to buy themselves one.**

A *Bart Simpson said, "It's just hard not to listen to TV. It's spent so much more time raising us than you have." You might need to spend time discussing your decision with them. Why not get them to read this chapter and blame us instead?*

7

The child-care minefield

Need two incomes to pay the mortgage or just can't stand the thought of being stuck at home 24/7? No family to look after the little one? You need child care.

For many couples and single parents, the option of one parent being at home looking after the kids isn't on the agenda. Bigger and bigger mortgages or rents, utility bills, and lifestyle necessities ensure that fewer families now have a full-time parent. And even when this might be possible, more and more parents are reluctant to abandon a career and training they have worked so hard to achieve.

Many of our friends feel that finding suitable people to look after their kids when they're at work seems more stressful than their children ever are. Great child-care providers, however, are worth their weight in gold and make a huge difference in your children's quality of life.

Here's an idea for you...
Sometimes you chance across an earth mother whose passion for her own and everyone else's children is evident. She may seem an ideal candidate but it has never occurred to her to become one or she is put off by the forms involved in registering with the state. If she is interested, why not make inquiries? Help her with the application or put her in touch with a professional child-care association. It takes time and energy on your part but the peace of mind knowing that a domestic goddess is caring for your children makes it a price worth paying.

Whether you need someone to look after the children from the time you both leave for work in the morning until you get back at night, or just someone to take your children to school or daycare, here are a few proven ways to make things easier.

RESEARCH

Time spent researching is well rewarded. Just because Penelope is a registered provider doesn't mean she's right for your kids or you. Personal chemistry is vital. Can you all get along? Will you be able to resolve conflicts? Are her thoughts and feelings about child rearing more or less similar to your own? Then there are practical considerations, like whether it's possible to get the car to her place when the roads are choked with moms doing the school run. Will she mind looking after your two-year-old into the evening if you get stuck in the office unexpectedly? And can you agree on a fee that keeps her happy without you needing a second mortgage?

We suggest that you sit down and plan your hunt for the ideal child-care provider with military precision. Find as many candidates in your area as you can. Be nosy. That way you won't end up leaving your vegan children with a butcher's wife. Prepare a questionnaire that includes questions about the caretaker's personality, how she relates to your child, what other members of her family feel about these interlopers, evidence of toys and other stimulation, and what structures are in place. Some caretakers run their service like mini-nurseries, with cooking and painting sessions, while others just plonk pre-teens in front of the TV until you return. The more candidates you see, the more likely you'll find one best suited to your needs.

Kids giving your child-care provider a hard time? Have a look at IDEA 16, *Spare the rod*, and IDEA 18, *Nursery crimes*, for ways to break the deadlock.

Try another idea…

MONITOR PROGRESS

It is vital to build up a good working rapport with caretakers. Short reports identifying problems and good things ensures that difficulties can be resolved at an early stage and positive behavior reinforced. It is important to listen to and observe your children as well. Sally, aged three, became depressed and started wetting herself at her caretaker's. Her parents couldn't understand this, as she had been continent since she was 15 months. It turned out that Sally was the only child in the house and ignored by the caretaker, who spent all the time in the kitchen smoking and drinking coffee with other moms with school-age children. Sally had found that wetting herself was a wonderful way of getting much-needed caretaker's attention.

REVIEW PROGRESS

The relationship your child has with her caretaker is dynamic. Things change. We have known caretakers who were delighted to look after other people's kids when their children hadn't started school, as it provided them with playmates. The same earth mothers became resentful of the commitment of having to look after other people's pre-teens during school hours once their youngest started school. Others are great with babies, yet not so hot with four-year-olds. It helps to have regular meetings, say, once a quarter, to review progress.

KEEP TO THE LETTER OF YOUR CONTRACT

Make a contract with your child-care provider detailing everything that is relevant: extra money for late arrival, cell phone number where you can be contacted in an emergency, formal notice of times you will be dropping off and picking up the kids, date and payment method. Stick to your side of the contract, however angry you feel. Looking after other people's children is not an easy task and people with skill who perform this vital function need to be cherished and valued when they do a great job. Get it right and you'll feel a whole lot better about having to go out to work.

Q   On the last couple of occasions that I've picked up my little girl
from daycare, she has burst into tears as soon as she sees me,
making it clear how much she hates being there. The caretaker's
son is rather rough with her at times and the caretaker dismisses
my daughter's distress, saying she is just making it up. I'm
inclined to believe my daughter, however. Generally, we think it is
a good and friendly home. What should we do?

How did it go?

A   *Tricky one. On the one hand children will always get into fights with others
and your daughter is being prepared for school, yet if she feels that you
and the caretaker are ignoring her distress she'll feel that you are not
taking her seriously. We suggest that you sit down with the caretaker and
talk it through to see if there really is a problem and how it can be
resolved. If she doesn't want to know, perhaps your daughter would be
better placed elsewhere.*

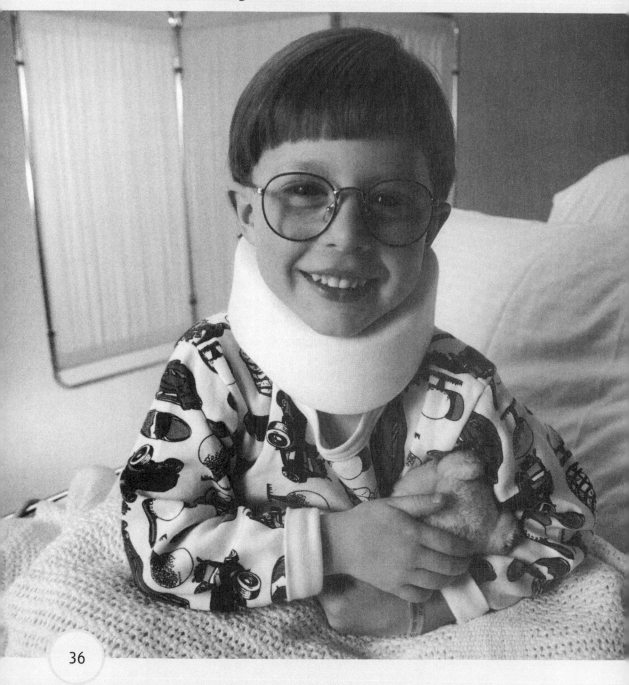

8

Safe as houses

Life's hard for toddlers. Curiosity and clumsiness is a challenging combination. Toddler-proofing your home allows them to explore freely while developing a strong sense of trust in you, themselves, and their environment.

As anyone who has a toddler knows, they are inquisitive creatures with limited danger awareness, always looking for new and exciting places to explore. Toddlers are also impatient and willful—characteristics that are potentially dangerous when fueled by their questioning nature.

No parent can watch a toddler all the time, but you do need strategies for reducing risks from ordinary household hazards, so your children don't get hurt when your attention is momentarily diverted.

Here's an idea for you...

Take your children shopping to try safety gates out before you buy them. Some models look good, but quick-witted children can open them easily. Remember that safety gates commonly placed at the top and bottom of stairs can also be used in doorways to prevent access to an off-limits room, for example a study or if you are decorating.

A TODDLER'S-EYE VIEW

Other parenting books advocate crawling around the room at toddler height. We think you need to get into a toddler's mind. For example, you see a bookcase. A toddler sees a ladder. What can you do? Forget about making it a safe bookcase and concentrate instead on making it a safe ladder. Will the shelves hold your toddler's weight? Can you fix it to the wall? Would it fall if a three-year-old climbed to the top? In our experience, parents make toddlers' bedrooms safe, placing cribs and beds away from windows and curtains, which deters budding climbers, and putting childproof locks on windows. But let's take a tour of the rest of your home. You'll probably have guards on electric outlets within your child's reach, but it's also worth including outlets that can only be reached by standing on accessible furniture.

Bathrooms

You can eliminate most bathroom accidents by using non-slip rugs, taking the lock off the bathroom door and replacing it with an eye hook and elastic band, locking medicines away in a high cabinet, and using a water thermometer when preparing a child's bath.

Kitchen

Do you have safety locks on cupboards and drawers, especially the ones where you keep sharp implements? Most parents know to store cleaning supplies and bleach out of reach, but dangling appliance cords can be harder to hide. Wrap them as short as is practical and secure with a tight elastic band. Instead of a kitchen tablecloth, why not consider a non-slip table covering instead? Not only will your toddler be less able to pull it—along with the table's contents—down on her head, but she'll also have a more suitable surface for drawing and making things.

> *"The most important emotional accomplishment of the toddler years is reconciling the urge to become competent and self-reliant with the longing for parental love and protection."*
> ALICIA F. LIEBERMAN, psychologist

Defining idea...

Living room

You know those soft corners for sharp furniture edges? We don't like them. They're often difficult to secure and just too tempting for toddlers to chew. If you have a coffee table with sharp edges, you don't have to get rid of it; just cover the corners with bubble wrap or pipe insulation material and masking tape until your navigator is older. If a table has a sharp edge all around its perimeter, why not use a duvet instead of a tablecloth? Your friends might laugh at your sense of interior design but your children will never have bruised foreheads.

Our friend had a decorative mimosa plant that looked like a tasty snack to her toddler. Soil or decorative stones from the base of a potted yucca might also pass for culinary treasure. We don't need to remind you to check that houseplants within reach are not poisonous, but bear in mind that even non-toxic plants may have dangerous spikes or small leaves that toddlers could choke on.

Try another idea...

If you want to teach your child to avoid danger (and distressing breakages all around), it's no use shouting at her. IDEA 16, *Spare the rod*, talks about how to teach children to be good.

Try to create at least two clear paths through the room so children can move easily and safely. Bear in mind that brothers and sisters in the same family can be different. Just because little Johnny wasn't curious about your Hummels doesn't mean little Jenny won't be. Move vases, antiques, collectibles, and other items of sentimental value away from low shelves and other accessible areas until your children have learned both to understand the word "no" and have good coordination. Again, you might like to shorten long appliance cords, especially table lamp cords. Many toddlers find it fun to pull small lamps off occasional tables.

Beware breakable windows, glass ornaments, TVs, glass-topped coffee tables, and free-standing lamps that toddlers can push over. Although most upright lamps are too light to hurt your toddler if they land on her, the bulb often shatters into countless little pieces of sharp glass that are unkind to small feet and the person responsible for picking them up over the next decade.

Garage
Garages and sheds are full of dangers for toddlers. Weedkiller, cans half full of paint, power tools, pliers, handsaws, slug pellets, chicken wire, and a lawn mower can all cause serious problems in the wrong hands. One solution is to make garages and sheds "no go" areas for toddlers. Alternatively, your toddler could be an incentive to sort out what you need and throw the rest away. Treat yourself to some new, toddler-proof, storage boxes to organize everything, and your toddler can play safely.

Q   **We have childproof locks on all our kitchen cabinets, but my wife keeps nagging me to put cleaning materials in high cupboards anyway. Is she being overanxious?**

How did it go?

A   *Your wife's right. We have yet to see a lock that is truly childproof. All the ones we've come across just take children longer to break into.*

Q   **How do I know if my three-year-old is big enough to sleep in a bed without falling out?**

A   *Check if he can climb up and down from the bed without any difficulty. Try letting him have a daytime nap on the bed first, when you can watch him sleep. If he manages without falling or rolling out, he probably doesn't need a guard anymore.*

9

Are we there yet?

Do long car journeys with your children drive you crazy? With a bit of pre-planning, the whole family can enjoy rather than endure them. Instead of dreading long trips, you'll soon look forward to spending time in the car with your children.

Unlike a train, plane, or even ferry, car journeys are everyday experiences for children and lack novelty. Add that they are strapped in and have limited visibility, and it's easy to see why so many kids hate this mode of travel for anything but short trips. But long car journeys can be made into exciting adventures.

Involve children as much as possible. Why not let everyone pack their own lunchbox? Little children could choose a small toy or book. Get older children to map the route and take turns navigating, looking for signs and place names. Make sure everyone visits the bathroom before setting off and at rest stops, as this saves

Here's an idea for you...

If the weather is good, why not plan a picnic at one of the rest stops? It's good for you, good for the children, and you'll have less food strewn around the car.

unnecessary stops. For younger children, pack a potty.

MUSIC ON THE MOVE

Everyone loves music. Unfortunately, everyone loves different music. While three hours of *Tristan and Isolde* might send you to Wagnerian heaven, it's likely to be hell for your family's heavy metal element. Compromise. Give everyone an allotted time to be DJ and introduce their favorite music for, say, twenty minutes. What about Desert Island Discs? Each member of the family has half an hour to play extracts from their all-time favorites and give a short talk on each of their selections. Alternatively, try Name That Tune. Whistle or hum the first few bars of a song while your children guess what it is. The first person to guess correctly hums the next tune. Sing-songs are the best low-tech way of passing time. But why stop at old favorites? Encourage children to be musically adventurous with rounds. Part singing is a skill that takes time to acquire and is fun. You might end up with your own gospel choir or barber-shop quartet.

GAMES AND PLOYS

Don't worry, we're not talking about miniature chess or jigsaw puzzles. There are no small pieces to lose under the car seats in any of these games. Make Backseat Bingo cards on your computer before you go. Instead of a card with numbers, children have to spot and cross off things they are likely to come across on the way, like a flock of sheep, service station, purple car, and specific town name. Make harder cards for older children and consider cutting pictures out of magazines for little ones.

In Just a Minute, members of the family have to talk on a given topic for sixty seconds without hesitation, repetition, or deviation. One point is awarded for a successful challenge. The challenger then talks on the topic for the remaining time. The person speaking when the minute is up wins two points and picks the next topic out of a paper bag.

Play Tall Tales. Start with "One day my family went on a car trip…" and take turns adding a sentence at a time. See who can keep a straight face the longest. If you are planning a longer break at a rest stop, pack some blank postcards. Keep children busy by letting them design their own postcards to send to friends when you arrive. Glue can be messy, so bring stickers and colored pens instead. It's useful to plan some quieter ploys, too, like listening to an audio book, so the whole family isn't worn out when you arrive.

FOOD TO GO

Chocolate melts. Sweets cause sticky messes. Chips make children thirsty. So what can you take to eat? Cubed cheese, sausage rolls, peanut butter sandwiches, carrot sticks, cucumber sticks, seedless grapes, pineapple chunks, berries, dried fruit, and juice go down well and rarely come back up. Give each child a sports bottle of juice. You'll have fewer spills.

Most children are happy with the food choices we have suggested. But if they complain or are picky about eating, don't let it spoil your journey. Take a look at IDEA 22, *Happy eaters*: you might find that techniques suggested for the dinner table are just what you need in your car, too.

Try another idea…

"Everything in life is somewhere else, and you get there in a car."
ELWYN BROOKS WHITE (1899–1985), essayist and literary stylist

Defining idea…

45

How did it go?

Q **Why did my children lose interest in Just a Minute and start arguing?**

A *It sounds as if they got bored. When children are bored, they bicker. Next time try changing to a new game while they are still enjoying the current one. Stopping while they want more prevents boredom. Alternatively, take a rest stop for everyone to calm down. Distraction is sometimes the best tactic. If frequent arguments are a problem, take a look at Idea 3, Squabbling siblings.*

Q **Why don't my children listen to audio books? They just talk over them.**

A *Concentrating for a whole audio book can be too much for some children. Try playing tapes in shorter bursts, like 10–15 minutes, and discuss what they have been listening to. Ask them about their favorite character and what will happen next. Set up suspense between installments.*

Q **Our children become overexcited and hyperactive. How can I get them to calm down?**

A *Small children seem to fall asleep easily in cars, but older children generally don't. If it's getting close to bedtime, or if things are getting too lively, play Statues. Everyone sits as still and quietly as possible. Whoever sits still for longest wins a little present. For other quieting down games, see Idea 15, Generation games.*

10

A book at bedtime

Books breed brilliance. Parents who read raise pre-teens who succeed. A minor investment, just twenty minutes a day, will bring major returns.

If you read to your children, they'll have better concentration, longer attention spans, richer imaginations, increased independence, enhanced written and spoken communication skills, and the greatest range of choices and opportunities.

Fostering a love of books in your child or children could be your greatest legacy. Nothing rivals reading for its ability to develop your child's imagination and increase his or her vocabulary, the building blocks of thought and communication. Books provide a flavor of worlds and periods of time, past and future, otherwise unavailable. Time spent reading to children every day not only develops literacy skills, but also strengthens emotional bonds and builds confiding relationships.

Here's an idea for you... **Why not buy the book of a film your family enjoyed? By necessity, film can only contain a fraction of the action or plot in a book and this additional material is a great way of extending the pleasure. This often leads onto reading other stories by the same author. Watching *Babe* could prepare your young readers to discover the whole of Dick King Smith's canon.**

Defining idea... **"If you learn to read you are never bored and are never boring."**
PAULINE QUIRKE, actor (mother of two)

OFF THE SHELF

As you know, children are more influenced by what we do than what we say. There is no point in going on about the virtues of books and the wonders of literature if your children only ever see you slumped in front of the TV until you fall asleep. If, on the other hand, you have a varied and well-thumbed selection of books on your shelves, children will explore. Your daughter may find she prefers boy's action books rather than pony stories, but she won't make this discovery without access to books. Want to buy books but short of money? Thrift shops sell children's books much more cheaply than secondhand bookshops. Keep a look out for lots of books on online auctions. And encourage family and friends to give books as presents instead of money.

START EARLY

Reading to your baby may sound crazy, but is it? In a way it doesn't matter what you read. Your baby may not understand the words but quickly latches onto the subtext: time and attention from Mom or Dad. And what could be sweeter than music from a mother's mouth? Words, tone, intonation, syntax, and grammar may be mere sounds at this stage but everything is being processed and ought to give your child the start in life that every parent hopes for.

TODDLER'S READING

Introduce a special corner for reading, with squishy cushions and good lighting. If toddlers associate reading with other valued items like a comfort blanket, you're onto a winner. Toddlers should be involved in choosing books. Even at this age there is a staggering array of books to select. We believe books should be objects of desire, so look for books with unusual textures, bright colors, and squeaks or other sounds. Plastic waterproof books are good for bathtime, but also very useful for teething toddlers to chew on. When you read to your toddler, bring stories to life by making sound effects and funny voices, and encourage him to copy you, turn pages, and chat about what is happening.

PRE-SCHOOL

Take your child on a special outing to join a junior library and let them spend an afternoon looking at the range of titles. Show them how to take books out but let them make the final selection. Make library trips a routine event at least every three weeks and take advantage of special events like opportunities to meet children's authors or visiting storytellers.

Some children say they don't have time to read anything other than schoolbooks. Most watch around twenty hours of TV every week, and are unable to find twenty minutes a day to read. Sound familiar? Take a look at IDEA 6, *Turn off the TV*.

Try another idea...

"There is more treasure in books than in all the pirates' loot in Treasure Island. *Best of all, you can enjoy these riches every day."*
WALT DISNEY

Defining idea...

Defining idea...

"Children need to believe in powers outside themselves. That's why they read about witches and wizards and God knows what."
SEBASTIAN FAULKS, writer (father of three)

Defining idea...

"Fairy tales do not tell children that dragons exist. Children already know that dragons exist. Fairy tales tell children that dragons can be killed."
G. K. CHESTERTON

OLDER CHILDREN

Please don't stop reading to children once they have learned to read themselves. As far as possible, keep reading time sacred and avoid nagging about unfinished homework and household chores during those twenty minutes. Reading doesn't need to be restricted to books and stories. Comics, non-fiction books, and even magazines can all work their magic. Stick to your principle of reading what pre-teens select and you'll find opportunities for reflection and discussion.

Q   **Our older child doesn't want to read aloud anymore. What can I do to encourage her?**

How did it go?

A   *Continue reading to your other children. Make it clear that it is reading time, but don't nag. There is nothing wrong with silent reading alone. You could try reading some of the same books and spend time talking about them.*

Q   **My three-year-old wants me to read her the same story every night. It's driving me crazy and we have so many other great stories I could introduce. Any ideas?**

A   *Some kids are like this and it can be very annoying. It's part of normal language development. If you can't face the umpteenth re-reading of Goldilocks and the Three Bears, read it onto a tape and she can listen to it all day. She might be tired of it come reading time and be in the mood for something else. On the other hand, you might just have to press rewind.*

Q   **I can't get my four-year-old to sit still when I'm trying to read to him. Help!**

A   *Let him wiggle around if he wants, or stroke a pet (see Idea 28, All creatures grate and smell). Or you could choose books with short chapters or try a compilation of short stories to gradually build his attention span.*

Q   **The children's section of our local library is small and my nine-year-old son has read all the books. We can't afford to keep buying new ones.**

A   *It's great he's such a voracious reader. See if he can borrow books from another library. If he has a school library, they might make suggestions. Parents are often able to join libraries close to their workplace, where he could borrow books on your card. Do you have relatives in another town who might consider a similar arrangement? Advertise in his school newsletter to find children interested in book swaps.*

11

Tantrum taming

We hate to break it to you, but when it comes to your kid's tantrums you may be the cause. Get it wrong and they learn to control and manipulate. Can you be part of the solution? You bet.

Children who kick, scream and shout, "I want it now" in public can bring out the worst in all of us. That's why we often back down. But giving in teaches children tantrums work. Sadly, they don't grow out of this idea. Bad behavior worsens as these children get older.

There are ways you can avoid making tantrums worthwhile for children, while keeping them and others safe.

SMOOTH SAILING

What does your child get out of tantrums? It's important to know because if you change your response to stop them getting what they're after, tantrums stop. Most children learn to use tantrums to get their own way. If you say no sixteen times to

Here's an idea for you... **Learn to intercept. Planning to avoid tantrums means they happen less often. Generally, tantrums are more likely when children are tired, hungry, or overexcited. Record when tantrums happen. What time of day do they occur? What seems to precede them? What were you doing? What was your child doing? If you notice patterns emerging, experiment with daily routines and continue to keep the diary to monitor changes. If you don't immediately notice any patterns in the tantrum diary, make a note of bedtimes, mealtimes, and rest periods, and observe when tantrums occur. For example, midday tantrums might happen because your child has low blood sugar and is irritable. Introducing a mid-morning banana or having lunch an hour earlier could be the answer.**

Toddlers often throw fits because they are frustrated by all the things they cannot do. Offering choices makes them feel less helpless. If you have decided your son is having soup for lunch, try suggesting a choice: tomato or chicken. Don't ask if he wants soup for lunch unless you are prepared for him to say no.

your daughter's demands for a toy you cannot afford and the seventeenth time say yes, she learns she has the power to turn your no's into yes's.

Don't give in to children who have tantrums because they want something. The first time you say no to a request, give a brief explanation, like "No, you can't eat the chocolate mousse until you have eaten your dinner."

Children are persistent. They'll keep trying to get whatever they want, especially if previous tantrums have worked. Many have "monster" tantrums if "ordinary" tantrums aren't getting the desired reaction. Give in to a monster tantrum, and you're in trouble. You've taught your child that persistence pays, big-time.

DURING THE STORM

Before speaking to your child, take deep breaths and prepare your battle plan. It's impossible to reason with an out-of-control child. Crouch or kneel so you can look them in the eye and tell them it's all right to feel angry but not for anyone to get hurt. However angry or embarrassed you feel, try to speak calmly. Shouting, smacking, or grabbing children makes matters worse. Tell your child angry feelings don't have to take over. Explain you'll keep them safe. If she is kicking you, tell her you are going to hold her until she calms down, so that other people don't get hurt. Children are usually very scared when they are this out of control and being held can paradoxically be reassuring and comforting. When your child is calmer, take her to a quieter place to settle down. At home, she can go to her room, but in shopping centers a good place is either a diaper-changing area or your car.

AFTER THE STORM

Children often feel upset and shaky after tantrums. They need time to compose before trying to talk about what happened. Many are unable to explain or even understand what has happened. Deconstruct each tantrum into its

See IDEA 36, *Stress busters*. Even very young children can learn to recognize when they are getting angry or out of control and how to manage without having fits of rage.

Try another idea...

"I am not afraid of storms for I am learning to sail my ship."
LOUISA MAY ALCOTT

Defining idea...

"Children measure their own life by the reaction, and if purring and humming are not noticed, they begin to squeal; if that is neglected, to screech; then, if you chide and console them, they find their experiment succeeds and they begin again. The child will sit in your arms if you do nothing, but if you read it misses the reaction and commences hostile operations."
RALPH WALDO EMERSON

Defining idea...

component emotions. Think of them as anger plus at least one other emotion. When you find ways to help children with their emotions, they have less need to feel angry. For example, a frustrated child may need to be taught how to reach the toy shelf or have it moved lower, a jealous older brother may require more individual time, a girl afraid of the dark could be helped by introducing a bedroom night-light.

Handling tantrums is exhausting for you. Calm is said to come after the storm, but sometimes you'll need to go in search of it. Why not relax in the bath or go for a walk on your own?

How did it go?

Q **I had stopped letting him have his own way, but the other day my son screamed all the way through the supermarket for a chocolate bar and at the checkout I was so embarrassed by his screaming, I gave in and bought him one. How could I have reacted differently?**

A *Everyone has bad days. Put it behind you and start again. Just as it is difficult for children to give up their tantrums, it is difficult for parents to change their reactions to them, too.*

Q **I am trying to be firm with my children and not let them have what they want all the time, but my husband gives in when they shout because he doesn't like them making a fuss.**

A *Children need consistency from both parents or they will exploit differences, playing one parent off against the other. Take a look at Idea 19, Singing from the same song sheet, for more information. If this doesn't persuade your partner, stick with what you are doing. The children will behave better for you than him and this will probably be enough to change his mind.*

12

Grandparents: help or hindrance?

We'll help you find positives in even the most curmudgeonly and irritating couples. At best, grandparents can be wise friends, role models, family historians, sports coaches, and free babysitters.

Attitude is everything. Well, almost. Take our friends Sam and Harriet. Both their sons are grown up and, as far as they can tell, in happy marriages. But the reception they get in the two homes is completely different.

Harriet explains, "There's always a tense atmosphere when we go to Jamie's house. Jamie and Jo are polite and if you were there you wouldn't notice anything wrong. But whenever we offer to babysit, they reject it out of hand. Jo makes these snide comments that the grandchildren are picking up on. We send birthday presents and they never say thank you and we always get the feeling they are glad to see the back of us and are pleased to have done their duty. Den and Alice, on the other

Here's an idea for you...

Encourage your children to discover their history. Ask grandparents to photocopy letters, school reports, certificates, photographs, and marriage licenses. Unlike the originals, it won't matter if little hands leave marks. Next time grandparents visit, they can make a scrapbook with your children, preserving important stories and sharing their cultural and religious traditions. Children can add to this book as they grow older and meet other family members, perhaps interviewing them about their lives, memories, hopes, dreams, and regrets. Older children can make videos of these interviews, and include music from their grandparent's era. Another child can be assigned the role of family librarian, photographing and cataloging family heirlooms, recording dates of acquisition and biographies of previous owners.

hand, seem sad when we drag overselves away. They keep us involved, invite us to the kids' school plays, sports events, and other things. We end up spending so much more time with them. They're really pleased when we offer to babysit and the grandchildren come here for the occasional weekend."

Den and Alice seem to come up with solutions where all three generations win. So rather than taking their parents on vacation, thinking they'll be grateful and babysit every night, they see if they would like to have the kids over for a weekend every couple of months.

BUILDING BRIDGES

Grandparents are living history. They can connect your pre-teens to family narratives in many ways. A family cookbook, including recipes passed down through the family as well as newer favorites, can be a fun way to share memories. Peter's Aunt Gunnel has a recipe book that has been in the family for over a hundred years. She can remember her grandmother using it and now spends time making the same meals with her grandchildren.

IDEA GENERATION

Because they are not bombarded with them every day, grandparents are usually more appreciative of handmade presents. Not sure what to do with the clay flowerpot or papier-mâché pig your pre-teen made at school? Give it to granny. For an unusual present for granddad, why not help children make a family tree on a big pinboard with photos as well as names? You know pre-teens learn best by experience. And who better to learn from than enthusiastic teachers? Like pre-teens, grandparents don't have hobbies, they have passions. Let them give your children experiences you don't have time or the inclination for: fishing, knitting, developing photos the old-fashioned way, stamp collecting, or folk dancing.

Exchanging emails and digital photos can help pre-teens and grandparents feel connected. Not every granny is a silver surfer, so you might need to set up a time each week to phone instead.

FAMILY SECRETS

However open you are, there are some things children won't talk to you about. Several children we know had problems getting along with their parents, and advice from their

Maybe your kid's grandparents live far away so they can't see each other very often. They may have trouble maintaining their relationship during long absences. If so, try some suggestions in IDEA 42, *Part-time parents.*

"If nothing is going well, call your grandmother."
ITALIAN PROVERB

"Nobody can do for little children what grandparents do. Grandparents sort of sprinkle stardust over the lives of little children."
ALEX HALEY, writer

"The reason grandparents and grandchildren get along so well is that they have a common enemy."
SAM LEVENSON, comedian, author of *Sex and the Single Child*

"It is one of nature's ways that we often feel closer to distant generations than to the generation immediately preceding us."
IGOR STRAVINSKY

grandparents helped enormously. Who else knows those difficult parents better? Grandchildren also offer parents a great incentive to put past difficulties behind them as pre-teens act as an unknowing catalyst, uniting parents and grandparents with a mutual object of love and admiration.

How did it go?

Q   As a family we get along well with my wife's folks but not mine. Any suggestions to improve matters?

A   *Why not use a family meeting? See Idea 29,* Order, order, *to brainstorm solutions. The ideas you come up with will work better than ones we suggest, as we don't know your parents. As a guide, focus on how you spend your time together and how you could make your parents feel more valued. You might want to buy some games and toys to leave at your parents' place. If children have fun there, they'll be more likely to want to go back.*

Q   My parents live abroad. I need a practical way my children can stay in touch with their grandparents.

A   *Speak to your parents about long-distance gardening. It works like this. Whenever they plant anything, get them to send your children a few of the seeds they used. Your children can send photos of how their seedlings are growing and share stories. This works even if you live in a high-rise building. Your children can use pots on the balcony or windowsill instead.*

13

And so to bed

Chances are, your pre-teens have a range of tactics to avoid going to bed and staying there. But even if they've won previous slumber wars, you can now outwit them with the ultimate bedtime battle plan.

Sleep is sacrosanct. Children who don't settle or sleep through the night affect the morale of the whole family. Sometimes sleep problems seem insurmountable. Everyone resigns themselves to living in a state of sleep deprivation. Nodded off during your appraisal meeting with your company director?

A consistently applied bedtime routine coupled with strategies for dealing with pre-teens who get up or cry in the small hours can turn things around. Still not convinced? Pre-teens who sleep well do better at school, have fewer colds, and are more creative and less irritable.

Defining
idea...

"Never leave a baby alone to cry. This is an absolute rule. He may be crying because he is hungry, cold, too hot, or wet...But he may be none of these things; he may be crying because he is frightened, and if he is not reassured early this is a dangerous condition. If an infant...is allowed to remain frightened and alone, his first impression of the world into which he has come is that it is inhospitable, dangerous, and lonely and that there is no use seeking help...It is not a matter for surprise that such impressions may color his view of the world and the people in it permanently. Much of his subsequent conduct will be devoted to the object of making himself as secure as he can in an insecure world."

DR. M. BEVAN BROWN, psychiatrist and author of *The Sources of Love and Fear*

SEVEN STEPS TO SHUT-EYE

Before you yawn and skip this section, be warned. Implementing this basic bedtime routine can easily eliminate most sleep problems. If it sounds too good to be true, or too authoritarian, why not give it a try for a week?

1. Tell children when bedtime is approaching. Let them know an hour, then half an hour before. The trick is to mention it using a neutral tone, rather than letting it sound like a warning or threat, just as casually as you might say, "It's nearly lunchtime."

2. Introduce a bedtime alarm clock for small children or use a kitchen timer to ring at bedtime.

3. You know how hard it is to sleep after hectic activity. For pre-teens it's almost impossible. Your children should spend the hour before bedtime doing quiet activities.

4. The last half hour needs to be spent getting ready for bed: taking a bath, brushing teeth, and putting on pajamas.

5. Once they are in bed, read some nursery rhymes or sing a lullaby. Repetitive rhythms are soothing.

6. Make sure your child has his blanket and special toy.

7. Kiss her good night and explain you will see her tomorrow morning. Then switch off the light.

Exhausted your supply of nursery rhymes or poems? Sounds like its time to incorporate a daily story into the bedtime routine. Check out IDEA 10, *A book at bedtime*.

Try another idea...

CHILDREN WHO CRY AT NIGHT

Ignoring children who cry at night is stressful for you and them. Once you've found out why your pre-teen is crying, avoid staying longer than necessary or taking him into your bed. Some parents worry that if they ignore them, children will cry for attention. This hardly happens if children have enough individual time with you during the day. By praising good bedtime behavior you lessen the urge for attention-seeking crying.

CHILDREN WHO GET OUT OF BED

If children get up, put them back. Sounds simple, but is hard to do. Pre-teens come up with lots of reasons for getting out of bed: drinks, snacks, nightmares, and monsters. Conversations or cuddles can support their notion that getting out of bed is rewarding, so

"People who say they sleep like a baby usually don't have one."
LEO J. BURKE, educator

Defining idea...

Here's an idea for you...

Many pre-teens are early risers. A proven ruse that gets you an occasional respite is constructing snail trails between your children's bedrooms and yours. Each child follows their trail, punctuated by toys, games, puzzles, word searches, books, snacks, and drinks. If you get it right, it could take your children a stimulating hour to make this short journey. Prizes for correct puzzles help, especially if you throw in a couple of tricky questions.

try not to be tempted. Instead, praise them for something they are doing right, like going back to their room without a fuss. Keep this short, as long chats can encourage children to get out of bed in the future. If your pre-teen gets up regularly, explain during step 7 that if they wake up, they need to stay in their own bed.

THINGS THAT GO BUMP IN THE NIGHT

Frequent nightmares are usually due to stress or upsets like the death of a pet, moving, arguing parents, or bullying. You can help children who have scary dreams with gentle reassurance. Acknowledge problems, but tackle them during daylight.

Pre-teens sometimes have night terrors, sleepwalk, or talk in their sleep. These are worse in tired children. Night terrors are different from nightmares. Pre-teens with night terrors scream and although they look awake, they don't respond to you. Night terrors are distressing for parents, but children don't usually remember them, as they happen in a different part of sleep than nightmares, when children are more deeply asleep. The best thing to do if your child sleepwalks is keep his room safe and the floor clear of obstacles.

Q **I am not sure how to choose a suitable bedtime. My husband thinks the boys should be in bed by 8 p.m. but I think this is too early.**

How did it go?

A *Bedtimes need to be tailored to the age and sleep requirements of individual children, so it helps not to start with fixed ideas. For example, a two-year-old needs around thirteen hours of sleep, but this usually includes a couple of hours napping during the day, so at night he may need around eleven hours. A typical four-year-old needs twelve hours of sleep, whereas most ten-year-olds are content with ten hours. On non-school nights, experiment with different bedtimes. Are they tired the following day? If so, set an earlier bedtime.*

Q **Our daughter is scared of the dark and often comes into our bed saying she feels frightened. How can I get her to sleep in her own bed?**

A *Let her sleep with the light on in her room for a few days. Then leave the light on in the hallway, but keep her door open. After a week, tell her the door is going to be shut but she can still see a shaft of light under the door. At the same time give her a bedside lamp that she can reach to switch on from her bed and a night-light to plug into the wall so her room is never totally dark unless she wants it to be. If she comes into your room at night, take her back to her bed without letting her get into yours.*

Q   **My son will only go to bed if his dad reads him a bedtime story. Because he often works late, this isn't practical. What can we do?**

A   *Many children settle for one parent and not the other. Check that you both stick to the same seven steps. From now on, take turns to settle him on alternate nights, so when Dad next works late, bedtime isn't too different. If they have been reading a special story, read alternate chapters. Praise him for going to bed and ignore attempts to draw out bedtime. If you have been more lax with rules when Dad works late, for example, letting him stay up later, look at Idea 19,* Singing from the same song sheet.

14

Double trouble

Double trouble, toil and fuddle? Fertility treatments mean more moms are having multiples, but armed with these facts and tips, it can be twice (or thrice) as nice.

One of the biggest challenges parents face when raising multiples is how to develop each child's sense of individuality. Start by giving children distinct names. Jack and Philomena is better than Jack and Jill.

It's also better not to use names that will give children the same initials. Dressing them differently is another way of doing this. When twins are babies, people tend to give you two sets of identical baby clothes. Once they're older, let them choose their own. Sophie and David have twin boys. Friends often buy them identical presents: "Usually we keep one and take the other back to the store. We let them choose another toy in exchange. They learn to share and play together."

How do you know whether or not to buy two swings? Two kangaroo balls? Two sets of sandbox toys? We suggest you buy one of everything and review it after a few weeks. If you've found you really do wish you had a second swing, changing table,

Here's an idea for you...

As any parent who's ventured out of the house with their twins knows, strangers stop you in the street and ask "Are they twins?" After a while it gets overwhelming and exhausting. A snappy rejoinder like, "No, they were triplets but we misplaced one" will get the curious brigade off your back and leave you smiling rather than irritated.

Defining idea...

"It is not economical to go to bed early to save the candles if the result is twins."
CHINESE PROVERB

or mobile, you can always go back for it, but by waiting you'll save a lot of unnecessary duplication.

Whatever your intentions, even superhuman parents aren't going to be able to give twins the same level of individual attention afforded to singleton pre-teens. Some parents send twins to day care on different days, or arrange for one to stay with Granny while Mom spends the afternoon with the other. In some families, this helps twins build stronger relationships with parents and other members of the family, but it doesn't work for everyone. When some twins are separated, they miss each other desperately and talk about each other. Don't get too hung up, just let them be themselves. When people visit, they may need to be reminded not to ignore older single siblings while they're admiring your twins.

Our friend Tien hadn't expected to be pregnant. When a routine ultrasound showed twin girls, she was, in her own words, "hysterical." If this happens to you, once you've picked yourself up off the floor, consider taking maternity leave earlier than you'd planned and use this extra time to prepare. Instead of a baby shower, have a diaper shower. If everyone brings a pack of disposables rather than a bottle of bubbly you'll save lots of money. Once twins arrive, you'll be doing all the usual baby jobs. Twice. Midwives will tell you, "You'll need all the help you can get." So if your family lives far away or hasn't spoken to you since you hooked up with "that loser," you'll need to look elsewhere.

Twin toddlers can mean twice as many tantrums. For a bit of peace, check out IDEA 11, Tantrum taming.

Try another idea...

To meet understanding moms with seriously good local tips, join your local twin club. These international institutions provide opportunities to meet other multiple birth parents, swap news, and supply "trained volunteers" who visit you once or twice a week to play with older siblings or do practical things like shopping. Parents whose little ones are older than yours have been there, done it, and may even sell you the double stroller. It is also a great way for twins to meet other twins and have positive role models, which should make a pleasant change from being the odd (or should we say even?) ones out. An Internet trawl should reveal your nearest club or national organization.

"The best thing about being a twin is you always have a friend."
LARA MANDELL, twin, age four

Defining idea...

How did it go?

Q   **My twins are starting school this year and I'm not sure if they ought to be in the same or different classes. What do you think?**

A   *There's no evidence to suggest there are definite advantages of separating kids at a young age. Some schools have a policy of putting twins in different classes to encourage them to make friends with others and develop their learning independently. It probably doesn't do them any harm to be separate for lessons, as long as they can see each other at recess. We suggest you speak to your kids and do your best to accommodate their wishes.*

Q   **Our identical twins go to the same school and all the teachers mix them up. Their friends can tell them apart, but the teachers just don't get it. It really upsets them, as they're treated almost interchangeably. What can we do?**

A   *Why not meet their teachers and explain how important it is for the twins to be treated as individuals? Be up front and explain the telltale signs that you use to tell them apart. Do they have different postures, voices, or quirks? Alternatively, why not have a personalized necklace made for each girl? Nobody need ever mix them up again.*

15

Generation games

Games are a great way to pull the generations together.

Cards, Chinese checkers, chess, Clue...
or take your pick from our tested
selection.

WEIRD AND TWISTED

You need two teams of at least six players. It's more fun if they are different ages
and heights. The first team are the weird team. They stand facing a wall or fence, so
they can't see what the second, twisted team is up to. The twisted team join hands
and make a circle. Then the fun starts. They have to try and get twisted into a funny
shape, by stepping over each other's hands. They can't unlink hands, but anything
else is allowed. When they're truly twisted, the weird team has to untangle them,
without unlocking their hands.

THINK OUTSIDE THE BOX

Blindfold the first player. Have them put their hand inside an empty cereal box and
identify an object you've put at the bottom. Suitable objects include: marble,
toothpick, small doll, Play-Doh, piece of pasta, key, or rubber eraser. If your pre-teens
want to put objects in the box for adults to guess, take a sneak peek before Great
Aunt Nora has a heart attack correctly identifying Tommy's pet tarantula.

Here's an idea for you... **Everyone can play charades, where players use mime and the audience guesses a book, film, song, or play title, but why not try one-word charades? It's more fun, there are fewer hand signals to learn, and even little kids have a good chance of beating the grown-ups. Get them to act out single words like frog, door, circle, and candy. If you're hosting a themed party, prepare a list of suitable words for kids to pick out of a shoebox.**

SHADOWLANDS

A game for quieting down. You'll need to cover a wall with a white sheet. Pick a child who sits facing the sheet. Darken the room, but have a large flashlight handy. Invite people to walk in turn in between the light and the child. This child tries to identify people by their shadow. Encourage shadowmakers to distort their shadows by exaggerating features and making ears with their fingers. When someone is identified, he replaces the guesser.

BOXERS

A rough-and-tumble game played in pairs. Boxers face each other with their arms above their heads. Each holds the other's left wrist with their right hand. The aim of the game is to touch the top of your opponent's head without him touching yours. We recommend four one-minute rounds measured by a kitchen timer.

MEMORY

A quiet game for two to four players. You'll need a set of special cards in matching pairs. Put them all facedown in a random way, not in lines or anything like that. Take turns to turn two cards over. Anyone who finds a matching pair keeps them. If the cards are different, turn them back over and the next person has a turn. The winner is the person who has the biggest pile of cards at the end.

SNAP

Snap's an old favorite, but you can play it with the cards your pre-teens made for Memory. Two players have half the cards each. Put a card on the growing heap in the middle, faceup. When you have a card that matches the one on top of the pile, shout "Snap" at the top of your voice and keep the whole pile. The winner has all the cards.

THE JELL-O GAME

This is good for pre-teen parties, but also makes an unusual treat as a way of eating dessert after the kids have been good at the dinner table. If you can persuade elderly relatives to join in, it's even more fun. You need a large bowl of Jell-O, a die, two wooden spoons, and a pair of oven gloves. Working around in a circle, everyone rolls the die. When someone throws a six, she has to put on the oven gloves and, using the wooden spoons, take some Jell-O and eat it. While she's eating, remaining players still keep rolling the die. The next thrower of a six takes over. The bravehearted and those with tiled floors might like to blindfold the Jell-O eaters.

ALL AROUND THE WORLD

Another quirky quiet game. Sit in a circle or, if you're sitting in a car, work around the car. Choose someone (birthday boy, oldest male present, person who doesn't have a pet) to name a place. It can be a town, village, city, or country. For example, Paris. The next person names a place beginning with the last letter, like Spain, and so on. If a player can't come up with a place in the time it takes one of the other players to say, "All around the world," they're out.

To find out how pre-teens can make their own cards for memory and Snap, see IDEA 48, Arty facts.

Try another idea...

"In every real man a child is hidden that wants to play."
FRIEDRICH NIETSZCHE

Defining idea...

73

MOVERS AND GROOVERS

Unlike musical chairs, you don't need any special props and all the older grown-ups who have to miss out on musical chairs because of joint problems can join in this one. Place as many sheets of 8.5" × 11" paper as you have players on the floor. While the music plays, everyone weaves in and out of the paper shapes, in time to the music, but without touching them. Anyone who touches a sheet is out. When the music stops, players jump onto the closest paper. Only one person can stand on each sheet. Take one paper away after each stop, and the person left without a piece to stand on, is out. You can theme paper shapes depending on the type of celebration: hearts for Valentine's parties, flags for Fourth of July, or moon shapes for a slumber party.

FIZZY FIZZ FIZZLERS

An outdoor "getting to know you" game for a group of eight or more. One person is a fizz and has a bouncy ball. The fizz throws her ball and calls out another player's name, say Susan. Susan comes and gets the ball. Everyone else runs away from the fizz. When she picks it up, she says, "Fizzy fizz fizzler" as loudly as she can. When the other players hear this, they have to freeze. Susan can throw the bouncy ball at any of the other players, and if it hits someone, she shouts, "Fizz" and that person becomes the next fizz, who calls out a person's name while the others run for their lives.

Q   **Our son is seven. He's a middle child and has recently started cheating when we play Monopoly. Basically, he steals from the bank. We're worried this character trait might spread to the game of life. Help!**

How did it go?

A   *Perhaps you need to establish why he's cheating. Maybe he's unable to keep up, or bored with Monopoly? Play some games he has a chance of winning and see how it goes. You might like to check out Idea 18, Nursery crimes, but it doesn't sound as if you need to get heavy-handed just yet.*

16

Spare the rod

Smacked bottoms and slapped wrists might not have done you any harm, but they never teach children how to be good. Parents who are firm but cruel are missing a trick or three. Discipline the pain- (and guilt-) free way.

Like us, you may have been smacked when you were children. Maybe you feel it didn't do you any lasting damage. But most of us aren't sure if it did us any good.

You probably know slapping, hitting, or otherwise hurting children teaches them violence. But one of the greatest difficulties with smacking is that parents usually hit when frustrated after being pushed to your limits. And children lose respect if discipline is random or seems unfair.

NATURAL CONSEQUENCES

Natural consequences are what would happen as a result of your child's actions if you don't get involved. For instance, if little Ayub plays with a marble close to a drain, sooner or later it will roll down the drain and be lost. Try and use natural consequences whenever it is safe. If Sophie throws her rice pudding onto the floor, she loses her dessert.

Here's an idea for you...

Try changing how you speak to your children. Your aim is to tell them what you want them to do, rather than grumble about what they are doing wrong. So instead of yelling, "Stop shouting at once," try a comment like, "Please speak more quietly." Instead of, "Will you stop running," say, "Please walk slowly." Try turning every complaint into a request for an hour. Your pre-teen's response will amaze you.

Defining idea...

"My parents used to beat the shit out of me. And looking back on it, I'm glad they did. I'm looking forward to beating the shit out of my own kids, for no reason whatsoever."
DENIS LEARY, comedian and actor (father of two)

LOGICAL CONSEQUENCES

There are times when you can't use natural consequences because it would be dangerous; for example, if your daughter runs onto a busy road. In these situations, try logical consequences, in which you step in to correct dangerous behavior. "You must stay indoors until you have learned to play away from the road." Or if she persistently splashes large amounts of water out of the bath, pull the plug and end bathtime. Again, say something like, "When you have learned to keep the water in the bath, you can have a longer bathtime."

REDIRECTION

Sometimes children do something wrong because they have learned a new skill and are practicing it in the wrong place or at the wrong time. Redirect them. For example, your toddler may be pretending to mail something by pushing plastic building blocks into the rabbit's cage. Instead of slapping her hand away, redirection allows her to carry on practicing her new trick, but in a place where the rabbit won't get injured and she won't be bitten. Why not play post office and make a pretend mailbox out of an old shoebox? If your son is throwing antique books, play ball with him instead. When your daughter totters around in your best evening shoes, give her an old pair. Turn it into a game; rather than presenting them as second-best, decorate them with sequins or buy some dress-up clothes.

IGNORING

Not responding to naughty behavior works especially well when you suspect children are attempting to shock, upset, or aggravate you. Ignoring swear words, for example, is much more effective than making a big fuss or implementing a swear box, which usually breaks down when children run out of pocket money but keep swearing regardless.

SPANKING CUES AND TRIGGERS

Parents who've smacked before may well lash out again. Try to forgive yourself. Apologize to your child and explain that what you did was wrong. When you feel calmer, think about how it happened. Are there any warning signs? Some parents feel their face getting hot or their heart pounding. Once you identify your "spanking cues," use them as your cue to withdraw. Alternatively, there may be something your child does that acts as a trigger.

Before discipline becomes a problem, why not agree to certain rules? See IDEA 37, *Not in our house*, to learn how to involve the children in rule setting and what to do when rules are broken.

"In the little world in which children have their existence, whosoever brings them up, there is nothing so finely perceived and so finely felt as injustice."
CHARLES DICKENS (father of two)

"If you are short-tempered today, your children get spanked for every little thing they do. If you are feeling more tolerant, your children get away with murder. This inconsistency teaches children to be sneaky. It doesn't teach them right from wrong or how to make better decisions."
DR. SAL SEVERE, child psychologist and parenting expert

Defining idea...

"It is so easy to give a naughty boy a slap, overpower him in an instant, and make him obey, that in this world of hurry and distraction, who can possibly spend time to wait for the slow return of his reason and the conquest of himself in the uncertainty, too, whether that will ever come."
RALPH WALDO EMERSON (father of four)

Before the next time, try to plan an alternative way of responding.

WALK AWAY

Next time you think, "If she does that again I'm going to smack her," walk away. Tell her you need a few minutes to yourself and escape somewhere like the bathroom to calm down. It sounds simple but changing how we respond can be a steep learning curve and everyone has some bad days.

PRAISE

As a general rule, children hear a lot more criticism than praise, and many are left feeling bad about themselves. Children who feel better about themselves behave better. The challenge? To praise your children at least ten times a day. Once they realize they can get your attention for doing good, there will be less incentive for bad behavior. Look for and highlight good things your children do. In order for children to learn, praise needs to be specific. So instead of saying, "Good job doing your homework," aim for comments like, "Good job working quietly on your own for half an hour and letting your sister play on the computer."

Q **Sometimes my daughter is so out of control I smack her to shock her out of it. When she gets like that it is impossible to reason with her.**

How did it go?

A *It's impossible to reason with children when they are out of control. Instead of smacking, try Idea 20, Time out. It gives both of you a chance to calm down and resolve things.*

Q **I don't like spanking my son, but it gets his attention. Is it really such a bad thing?**

A *Spanking teaches him what you don't want him to do, but it can't teach him good behavior. He is likely to be so distressed afterward that it's impossible to have a conversation about what has happened, so he can't learn from his mistakes.*

Q **I recognize my "spanking cues" but I can't walk away when I feel like smacking my son because he is usually doing something dangerous.**

A *Pick him up and remove him or firmly guide him away from the dangerous activity. Don't try to reason or explain if you are angry or upset. Later, when you are both calmer, talk about what happened and why you had to remove him. When you can't physically walk away, you may need to mentally retreat to a quieter place. Have a look at Idea 36, Stress busters.*

81

17

Treats

**Teaching your kids good behavior? Don't trick, treat.
It won't spoil them and you can do it for free.**

Kids get treats for lots of reasons.
Sometimes as a reward for good behavior,
as a thank-you for looking after a little brother,
for doing extra chores, and sometimes as a way
of giving them attention when someone else in
the family has had a lot.

Jenny was treated to twenty minutes alone with Mom or Dad on the week when her brother was very ill so she wouldn't feel left out. Treats can also be used to motivate pre-teens to do well in spelling tests. It's good to give treats for lots of reasons, and sometimes for no apparent reason at all. When parents only use treats as rewards for good behavior, pre-teens learn to be good for things rather than for their own satisfaction, and also learn love is conditional on results.

REACH FOR THE STARS

Elsewhere we've suggested introducing star charts for dry nights in bedwetting pre-teens. Other families use them for kids who find it hard to complete homework or

Here's an idea for you...

Try the variable interval schedule with your pre-teens. Over the next couple of weeks, sometimes praise pre-teens at the start of homework time, at other times praise when they're halfway through homework, and the remaining times praise when they've finished homework. If we're right, you'll notice them sticking to their homework schedule better.

Defining idea...

"It is not giving children more that spoils them, it's giving more to avoid confrontation."
JOHN GRAY, *Children Are from Heaven*

Defining idea...

"Your children need your presence more than your presents."
JESSE JACKSON, civil rights leader, politician, and Christian minister

chores. They all work on a similar principle. Dry night, completed homework, or chore finished equals one star. An agreed number of stars can be cashed in for a treat. Run it by your accountant or at least a friend with financial expertise before you hand out half the solar system. And only promise what you can deliver. Carol promised her truant son a large amount of money if he went to school for a semester, and ended up having to get a second job to pay him.

In order to understand how kids learn, psychologists did some experiments with rats. Rats were given food pellets when they pressed a lever. Rats who were given a pellet every time they pressed the lever stopped pressing it when researchers stopped giving them pellets. They may not look it, but your pre-teens have a lot in common with those rodents. We've seen kids become star chart junkies, being good to cash in stars for big prizes, but reverting to old habits when the goodies ceased. Back to our rats. Psychologists decided to find out what effect giving pellets at different intervals would have on rats learning to press a lever. They gave some rats pellets intermittently, other rats were given a pellet every five times they pressed the lever, a third group of rats were given a pellet every five minutes, regardless of whether they pressed the lever or not.

The most effective pellet-giving schedule was what they called *variable ratio*. To you and us, this means rats who were given a pellet after pressing the lever, but they needed to press it a different number of times: Sometimes five presses would get them a pellet, sometimes seven, sometimes twenty-five. If it sounds too off the wall, just think of gambling. Adults buying lottery tickets or playing slot machines are subject to variable ratio reinforcement. Most of the time you don't win, but the possibility of a jackpot keeps you going. And the small wins along the way at unexpected times help reinforce the idea. Just like rats, pre-teens demonstrate consistently good behavior when their behavior is rewarded with treats unexpectedly.

CREDIT CARD IN CRISIS?

Treating your pre-teen doesn't have to mean splurging on the latest expensive toy that will be discarded when it's stopped being fashionable. Book and music gift certificates are available in small denominations. Instead of giving enough to cover the cost of a book, give smaller denominations, encouraging your child to save up for something specific, rather than little amounts of cash that get frittered away.

A packet of seeds is an inexpensive treat. See IDEA 32, How does your garden grow?

Try another idea...

"If you can give your son or daughter only one gift, let it be enthusiasm."
BRUCE BARTON, founder of advertising agency BBDO, creator of Betty Crocker

Defining idea...

"Four magic words, we can't afford it, should be part of every child's education... As exercise strengthens the body, frugality strengthens the spirit."
MORRIS MANDEL, author and public speaker

Defining idea...

In the Bradford household, whoever washes up earns ten minutes extra on the computer. Time spent alone with a parent is a treat when both of you work. One way could be to allow your child to choose an extra bedtime story. Some people advocate leaving little notes in kid's lunchboxes, saying "well done" or "Mommy loves you." Give this one a pass: in our experience, other kids in the class usually find them first and pick on the intended recipient. A better surprise treat to sneak into a lunchbox is a handful of strawberries dipped in chocolate. Extra time in the playground is a treat younger kids often like to work toward. Older girls like to be given a "professional" manicure by Mom. Choosing a video might be a double-edged sword if you have to sit through *Happy Feet* on a Friday evening. Instead, choose the film democratically and let the treat be making popcorn. Having a friend stay the night is a great treat for kids of all ages.

How did it go?

Q **My five-year-old daughter tries to save up stars for good behavior for special treats, but loses interest quickly and never gets there. She's really unmotivated. What can we do?**

A *When children are still very young, using treats as rewards like this works best if they have chances to earn a small treat soon after being good. Otherwise, they miss out on making a connection between good behavior and treats. Make it easier for her to earn small treats and she'll get the hang of it.*

18

Nursery crimes

Discovering one of your pre-teens has an appetite for pocketing things can panic parents. Caught stealing sweets and pleading innocence? How can you avert your artful dodger from a life of crime?

We'd be lying if we didn't tell you that all children lie. But why do pre-teens exaggerate, tell tall tales, or fib? Kristen, who is three, doesn't always know the difference between fact and fantasy.

Like many children her age, her tall tales give parents a glimpse of her wishes and imagination. Sometimes older kids lie because they want you to think they've been good or done the right thing. This might be to get a reward or avoid a sanction. Four-year-old Charlie knows he was wrong to eat his sister's lollipop, but doesn't understand the big deal about denying it. Older pre-teens are more likely to lie to save face; Jessica hasn't done her homework, so tells the teacher, "I left it at home."

You can stop pre-teens from lying by not giving them opportunities to do so. If you ask your son if he's stolen money from your purse when you've seen him do it, it sets him up to tell more lies. Pre-teens often lie when feeling cornered about a

Here's an idea for you... **We don't want to nag, but it might be useful to think about the sort of role model you are. If you come home every night and show off the pens, paper, and occasional laptop you've lifted from the office, don't be too surprised when lectures on honesty fall on deaf ears.**

Defining idea... *"On the whole, human beings want to be good, but not too good and not all of the time."*
GEORGE ORWELL

Defining idea... *"In automobile terms, the child provides the power, but the parents have to do the steering."*
DR. BENJAMIN SPOCK, pediatrician and child-rearing guru

misdemeanor. Next time you see your daughter with a piece of broken jewelry in her hands, instead of saying, "Did you break that lovely brooch Granny gave me? You know I've got nothing else to remember her by," try, "I see my brooch broke. Please tell me how it happened." As you know, pre-teens are mimics. If honesty is your best policy, it will be theirs, too.

We don't need to tell you that angry reactions like "If I find out you've lied to me, you'll be grounded until you're eighteen" make it much less likely pre-teens will come clean. If you're sure your child has lied to you let them know. "I don't believe you found that cell phone in your school bag. Please tell me where it came from." If your pre-teen is squirming, acknowledging it helps build trust: "I bet this is making you feel really uncomfortable, but I need to know the truth to help."

IT'S A FAIR COP

Your little cherub has fallen from grace, caught with his hand in the cookie jar and swearing he never took anything. It's not the first time, and you'd give him the benefit of the doubt, but he's guilty as charged. Many children go through an amoral phase when the impulse to own or consume something that isn't theirs becomes greater than the ability to resist.

Peter's little brother Arvid was caught stealing apples from a nearby convent. The nuns identified the miscreant and called the police. An enlightened policeman told Arvid and the other little hooligan that they had to apologize to the nuns in person. They did and were rewarded with a couple of the biggest, sweetest-tasting apples they had ever had. Neither ever stole again. The moral: Teaching children to own up and say sorry may be more important than punishing.

Think the punishment should fit the crime but not sure where to start? See IDEA 16, Spare the rod.

Try another idea...

"When people ask me what to do, I tell them to just give the child all the love they can. Don't worry too much about anything else. And when it comes to discipline, never, never, physically assault the child in any way, and certainly don't assault them with words, which can be just as cruel as physical punishment."
DR. ASHLEY MONTAGU, anthropologist and social critic

Defining idea...

"If there is anything we wish to change in the child, we should first examine it and see whether it is not something that could better be changed in ourselves."
CARL JUNG

Defining idea...

Many young pre-teens take things that do not belong to them because they are curious. We don't think it's helpful to call this "stealing" until they are old enough to understand that taking something that belongs to another person is wrong. Children under three don't understand about right and wrong. It's never too early to start teaching them though, so make lots of comments like, "That Ming vase belongs to Auntie Joan, so we'll find you something else to play with" or "Let's ask Arthur if you can play with his Legos."

But imagine your ten-year-old daughter has come home from school with a calculator you haven't seen before. You establish that it belongs to a classmate. We suggest you make her take it back and apologize. She will probably feel deeply embarrassed and guilty, but hopefully this will act as a deterrent in future.

How did it go?

Q **A couple of times recently, Denise, age eight, has taken money from my wife's handbag and bought candy. What should we do?**

A *Clearly, Denise needs to know that what she's doing is wrong and unacceptable. It might be a way of getting attention, so we suggest you explore what else is going on in her life. We think she should pay the money back, or do some of her mother's chores to pay it back that way. Experts have suggested that some children steal to replace something that is missing from their lives. Handled sensitively, you can change her behavior and sort out any underlying problems.*

19

Singing from the same song sheet

Doing it differently? Disagree about discipline? Return to perfect harmony.

We have different personalities, different childhoods, different genders, different assumptions, different expectations, different experiences, and different careers. It's hardly surprising we also have different parenting styles.

In harmonious relationships, parents accept and talk about differences; parenting styles become complementary and converge. When parents don't communicate effectively, or fall out, the opposite happens: Parenting styles diverge and become polarized. We've noticed the stricter parent becoming even stricter in response to a more permissive co-parent.

Georgia is a strict mom. Her routines are important. Without them, she feels, nothing gets done. Her partner, Martin, doesn't feel like domestic battles after a day in the boardroom. After all, he thinks, home is Georgia's turf. And because she has

Defining
idea...

"What matters to children is the way in which you present your differences, rather than the fact you have conflicting views. 'I would let you but Daddy won't,' may not be the most helpful approach."
ANDREA CLIFFORD–POSTON, child, family, and educational therapist

criticized his parenting, he feels useless and has almost given up. Most evenings, their children do things that Georgia disapproves of: eating sweets before dinner, doing homework in front of the TV, or refusing to clean out the hamster's cage. She cajoles, nags, and eventually ends up shouting. Then, in front of the children, Martin tells her off for being too hard on them. "They're only young once," he protests. And their kids? They love it, playing Georgia off against Martin, watching an entertaining argument and getting their own way.

Which parenting style is best? When it comes to raising children, democracy rules. In the 1930s, two researchers studied leadership styles by looking at groups of schoolchildren working on a mask-making project in different craft clubs. The groups had three types of leader:

- *Authoritarian*—this leader used orders to direct children's activities.
- *Democratic*—this leader offered guidance, encouraged children, and participated in mask making.
- *Laissez-faire*—this leader gave children information, but didn't become involved in their activities.

Let's look at what happened in each group:

Authoritarian

In these groups, researchers noticed two types of behavior: "aggressive" and "apathetic." Aggressive children were rebellious and demanded attention from the leader. They also blamed other children in the group when things went wrong. Apathetic children placed fewer demands on the leader and were less critical, but, when they were later given a non-authoritarian leader, tended to fool around. The children made more masks than the "democratic" group, but the quality of their masks was not as high.

Democratic

Morale was high, relationships between the children were friendly, as well as with the group leader. When the group leader left the room, children worked independently. They showed a fair amount of originality, and, although they produced fewer masks than the "authoritarian" group, the quality of their masks was higher.

Try another idea...

Do your children know what's expected of them? If your family's not clear about the rules, it's so much harder for parents to agree on sanctions and discipline. See IDEA 37, *Not in our house.*

Defining idea...

"Conflicting ideas about raising children have led to a breakdown in communication between mothers and fathers, despite their shared goal of rearing emotionally stable children who are prepared for the complexities of the world."
TINE THEVENIN, *Mothering and Fathering*

Here's an idea for you... **So your pre-teen has learned to play parents off against each other? Out-manipulate the manipulators by using "first past the post." The first parent to notice a broken rule or other misbehavior intervenes in his or her preferred way, no questions asked.**

Laissez-faire

This was the worst group. They did not produce many masks and those they produced were poor. Group satisfaction was lowest; they cooperated little and placed great demands on the leader, showing little ability to work independently.

MEET YOU IN THE MIDDLE

If parents recognize that they are becoming polarized, they can improve matters. Take our earlier example. As Georgia became more authoritarian, Martin became more laissez-faire. This was pointed out to them and Georgia took active steps to be less directive toward their kids. As a result, Martin started to take more responsibility for the children's behavior. It follows that when one parent becomes more democratic, the couple moves toward the middle ground.

CALL A CONFERENCE

When you disagree on discipline, instead of criticizing and undermining each other in front of the children, call a conference. Give each other ten minutes of uninterrupted time to outline how you see the problem and write a list of possible solutions. Identify pros and cons of each solution and set another ten-minute time limit to come up with a joint solution. When your pre-teens see you can disagree but amicably come up with a way forward, they learn powerful lessons in conflict resolution.

PHONE A FRIEND

We're convinced that sometimes we all need independent solutions from someone who doesn't have a personal stake in parenting disagreements. Wise friends who you both like and respect are great occasional sounding boards. Blood relatives may have an innate investment in one partner so a mutual friend may be better, but you know your family and friends better than we do.

WHAT DIFFERENCE WILL IT MAKE IF WE DO IT YOUR WAY THIS TIME?

In the heat of the moment, it's easy to feel that our way of doing things is best. Try to think ahead, not just to the end of the day, but far into the future. What difference will it make tomorrow, next week, or in thirty years' time, if just this once Dad lets them eat chocolate mousse instead of macaroni? Once he feels his parenting style is valued, too, he won't feel cornered and will be less extreme.

How did it go?

Q **My husband is very strict and inflexible about bedtime. I think that on vacation and weekends our kids should be able to stay up later.**

A *First, it's important to find out why your husband thinks it's important for the kids to be in bed. It might be that he thinks children of a certain age should get so many hours' sleep. Or maybe he's trying to make sure he has a few hours of quality time with you. Has he made such a stand that to capitulate would seem like a humiliating defeat? This issue can only be discussed away from the children and his reasons may be valid. The way forward will depend on what you discover. Maybe he'll agree to offer the children an experimental late evening one weekend in a way that lets him keep face.*

20

Time out

Naughty, not nice? Banish bad behavior in just five minutes.

No, we're not talking about locking your kids in the cellar. Time out means sending your pre-teen to a boring place for five minutes.

Pre-teens miss out on fun activities and company. Kids hate it, and will learn to do anything to avoid it. So they stop doing the bad things that land them there. Time out shows pre-teens that parents mean business.

TEN THINGS SMART PARENTS NEED TO KNOW ABOUT TIME OUT

1. Time out needs to be used to target specific things your pre-teen does that you have to change. In the trade we call them "target behaviors." For example, if you are going to use time out when your daughter hits people, don't use time out for swearing, too. Once you've decided to use time out for a target behavior, you'll have to stick to it.

2. Time out rooms need to be boring and safe. Guest bedrooms and dining rooms are usually suitable. Your pre-teen's bedroom is not. Whichever room you select, empty it of breakable objects or anything that looks like it might be fun to play

with. If you live in a small or open plan home, use a time-out chair in an area away from other kids and activities for time out.

3. The length of time children ought to spend in time out depends on the age of your pre-teens: 3–5 years, three minutes is enough; 5–10 years, five minutes; over ten years, ten minutes. Quality rather than quantity is key. Longer time outs are no more effective.

4. Once you've chosen your time out target behavior and location, it's time to tell your pre-teen. The best time to do this isn't when you're angry or to add color to a lively argument, but when everyone is calm and getting along reasonably well.

5. The way to sell time out to pre-teens is to tell them time out is something your family is introducing to help children behave better so they can feel better about themselves. Explain how time out works; for instance, sitting in the bathroom for five minutes.

6. It helps a great deal if you put a clock that kids can see in the time-out room and show them where the big hand will be pointing to at coming-out time.

7. It will all go horribly wrong if you use time out as a threat. For example, saying, "If you throw the hamster downstairs one more time, you'll have to go to time out" gives pre-teens an extra chance to do something bad.

8. Parents who use time out most successfully are those who plan ahead. When kids do target behaviors, time out follows like night follows day. Parents less successful with time out tend to be inconsistent, for example, letting kids off sometimes and other times losing it and shouting, "You look like someone who wants to be in time out."

"When my kids become wild and unruly, I use a nice, safe playpen. When they're finished, I climb out."
ERMA BOMBECK

Defining idea...

9. Time out won't work if you use it in isolation. Look at IDEA 16, *Spare the rod*, for other strategies to try in conjunction.

10. Using time out at home and it's working well? Great, but what do you do when you're out and about with your pre-teen? Some parents get around this by making a note of any misbehavior usually resulting in time out, and sending the child there immediately when they get home. The problem with this is that there is inevitably a delay between misbehavior and time out, and your pre-teen may continue to act out during the outing, knowing she will be going to time out anyway when she gets back. If you're in a shopping mall, park, or place of worship, there will usually be a quiet area, like a mother and baby room or even an outdoor bench where your child can sit quietly for five minutes. If you're in a restaurant or fast-food outlet, a baby-changing area will be your best bet for younger children, but you may need to take an older child outside for five minutes.

How did it go?

Q   **My son calls out "How many more minutes?" about four times a minute. Because I have to keep going to tell him, he ends up getting more attention than when he's not in time out.**

A   *You're right that paying him extra attention will make time out counterproductive. Kitchen timer, egg timer, hourglass clock—tell him you will tell him when the time is up, not before.*

Q   **My daughter screams and has tantrums during time out. What can I do?**

A   *We know it's tough, but the best strategy is to ignore her. If tantrums are a problem at other times, check out Idea 11, Tantrum taming. Don't start counting minutes in time out until her tantrum is over. Tell her she has three minutes in time out and you'll start timing when she's quiet. Once she has learned that silence gets her out of time out quickly and tantrums extend it, she'll stop screaming.*

Happy trails

Mom's desperate to relax and rejuvenate, Dad's hankering after a hip hangout, but your pre-teens' perfect vacation is playing, pestering for pricey souvenirs, and protesting about funny foreign food. Make three wishes and you'll be on your way to the happiest vacation ever.

We blame the tour operators. Glossy brochures sell you a dream: long, deserted beach, warm sea, cocktails, and kids' club. The reality: hotel still being built, beaches overcrowded, and kids' club run by a college kid with neither the talent nor inclination necessary to occupy pre-teens while you read your novel and sip sangria.

How can you turn the tables on travel agents? By booking your next family vacation knowing what you'll need to keep the whole family happy. It all starts when you make three wishes. We know, it sounds like a fairy tale, but a fairy tale vacation wouldn't be a bad thing, would it? Ask everyone in the family to come up with

Here's an idea for you... **Pre-teens' ears can become very painful when adjusting to changes in cabin pressure, particularly during takeoff and landing. Sucking on a bottle or straw of a juice box helps. One more thing: Once toddlers have tired of looking out of the window, they can usually be kept busy for a while by asking them to clean the window with baby wipes.**

three wishes that would make it a perfect vacation for them. Older siblings and parents may feel a bit too grown up to make wishes, so ask them, "How will you know when we get back that you had a good time?" and get them to whittle this down to three responses. Once the whole family has made their wish lists, compare notes. We think you'll be amazed at the amount of overlap. The Ashworths usually book a cheap package holiday by the seashore and hope the kids will enjoy the beach club. "Last year we realized it just wasn't working," said Melanie. "I wanted to relax on the beach, my husband wanted to explore and play tennis, and the kids wanted us to make endless sandcastles. I ended up bribing them, 'If you just let Mommy lie still in the sun for half an hour, I'll play with you all afternoon.'" Everyone ended up unhappy and resentful. So they did it differently.

Defining idea...

"We all need time to dream, time to remember, and time to reach the infinite. Time to be."
GLADYS TABER (1899–1980), writer

The Ashworths each wrote down three things that would make their vacation perfect. They agreed to plan the trip around the most popular wish and to do at least one of everyone's wishes for at least one day of the trip. All three children wanted somewhere to play that was different from home, with different games or activities, and wished their parents would have time for them. Their mom's wishes were for a bar, a babysitter, and a beach. Swimming was on everyone's list, so they made that a priority. They went to Iceland and most of the holiday was spent swimming in the Blue Lagoon. They stayed in self-catering apartments, so they could eat what and when it suited them. The children played on an indoor jungle gym while their parents relaxed in the rooftop Jacuzzi. Dad spent two days scuba diving, while Mom played with the kids. Mom spent a couple of days being pampered in a thermal spa. On Saturday evening, the children went to a kid's film club while their parents went to a cool bar. They all agree it was the best vacation they've ever been on and would never have chosen that destination before.

Pre-teens can make a message in a bottle in a few moments, maybe while you are getting ready and they're clamoring to go out. Here's how: Scrub the label off an empty glass wine or water bottle, write a short message, and add their name and email address. Cork the bottle, seal with a dollop of candle wax or plumbers tape. Later, when you're walking by the beach, let them throw it into the tide. No beach? No problem. They can also be sent off downstream or launched into a river. Your kids might have a letter from the finders waiting when you get home.

Here's an idea for you...

Traveling with pre-teens needn't be a nightmare. See IDEA 9, *Are we there yet?*

Try another idea...

DON'T FORGET YOUR TOOTHBRUSH

If you're looking for a packing list, you bought the wrong book. You know your family and the sort of vacation you're going on, so we don't think it's our place to tell you if your kids'll need Ts, hoodies, belts, bikinis, woolly mittens, or retro wraparound shades. We will say this though: Bees and wasps are attracted to flowery patterns (no, we can't figure it out either) while malaria-spreading mosquitos like anything blue.

 How did it go?

Q   When we go away with our pre-teens, the only thing they eat without coercion is fries. We're going to Greece this year. How can we get them to eat local food?

A   *As you know, pre-teens love routine. Prepare them for going away by taking them to a Greek restaurant, or at least pop in to your local kebab shop so they can eat something they recognize when you get to Greece.*

22

Happy eaters

Are your kids fad eaters or junk-food junkies? We'll help you rustle up something to make your pre-teens cheerful chompers.

We are what we eat. We become what we have eaten. Exercise comes into the equation, of course, but it's the meals we eat and especially the meals we eat between meals that count. This is truest when we are young. The food we eat then has a bearing on the shape of what's to come.

RECIPE FOR SUCCESS

Entrées

Food fads are common in young pre-teens and usually pass quickly. Toddler Tim refused to eat anything but yogurt for three days. His mom, Tricia, handled it well by not making a big deal of it. In the end he succumbed to some jam sandwiches that she cut with a heart-shaped cookie cutter. Older fussy eaters can cause more problems. You can reduce conflict by offering choice. To avoid preparing meal

Here's an idea for you...

Worried about the additives in prepared meals? We don't feel like cooking every day either, but have found that by doubling quantities when we do cook and freezing leftovers, the freezer's always full of homemade meals, ready to go. If raisins, dried fruit like mango strips, seeds, and nuts are easily available and there is always fresh fruit like a bowl of shiny plums available, the temptation for chips or sweets is diminished. That way you can stick to your resolve of making junk food an occasional treat rather than a convenience.

Defining idea...

"Ask your child what he wants for dinner only if he's buying."
FRAN LEBOWITZ, writer and wit

Defining idea...

"There is no finer investment for any community than putting milk into babies."
WINSTON CHURCHILL

after meal for a picky eater, negotiate a choice before you cook. Offering two equally nutritious choices shows you are prepared to compromise.

Starters

Children who eat breakfast do better at school. They're less tired later in the day and their concentration is better. All pre-teens have days when they're simply too sleepy for a bowl of cereal. Give them a banana and little box of raisins to eat on the way.

Nouvelle cuisine

As you know, pre-teens like routine. When they're tired of lasagne, they're tired of life. Some are enthusiastic about new foods, but many are wary. So how do you smooth the transition from fishsticks and fries to salmon filet and linguine? We suggest you introduce one new food at a time, as part of a favorite meal. Try adding olives to their best liked pizza topping. Or pass off a new ingredient as familiar food. Ostrich cheeseburgers, turkey mince spaghetti bolognese, and crabmeat fishcakes should get you started.

Table manners

If you want your pre-teens to have good table manners, start young and make a game out of it. Trace a dinner plate on a piece of paper and also draw cutlery in, as if you were setting a table. Get your kids to color their "plates" and have them laminated. Using these personalized placemats, even little children can set the table, as they provide such a strong visual cue. If your kids talk with their mouths full, teach them not to by ignoring questions that leave you splattered in ravioli. Once they notice you answer siblings who speak after they've swallowed, they won't need nagging.

Sweet talking

In Finland, children have a designated "sweet day" every week. They have to save up any sweets they buy or are given on other days. We realize this "feast or famine" approach isn't for everyone, but why not have a designated "sweet time," like after dinner or as a treat after finishing homework?

Try another idea...

Why not get children cooking when they are very young? You can start them off with simple tasks like sprinkling cheese on spaghetti bolognese, and when you're baking they will love licking the raw ingredients off spoons and bowls and making their own mini buns. Pre-teens bored of the same old sandwiches in their lunchbox? **IDEA 43, *Little chef*, should satisfy the most demanding of appetites.**

Defining idea...

"The golden rule of raising babies. LIE. Lie to your mother, lie to your sisters and aunts, and above all, lie to all the other mothers you meet in the street. When a newer mother than you asks for your help, tell her you never had the least trouble. Your baby just loved his mashed bananas on the first try."
ELINOR GOULDING SMITH, *The Complete Book of Absolutely Perfect Baby and Child Care*

107

How did it go?

Q **Our three-year-old manages to make meals last hours; it's a fight over every mouthful. We never had this trouble with his older sisters.**

A *Why not try time-limiting mealtimes? Say twenty minutes and time him using a kitchen timer. You will have to warn him beforehand but remove his plate when the twenty minutes are up. Once he sees that you mean business, the war of attrition will be over.*

Q **Claire, six, never finishes what I put on her plate. It's such a waste. What can I do?**

A *You could give her smaller portions. If she complains that she is getting less than her younger brother you can offer to give her second helpings once she has eaten the first serving.*

Q **Our daughter won't eat broccoli and refuses most other green vegetables. She's eleven and we thought she would have grown out of her food pickiness by now.**

A *Relax. Kids who don't eat cabbage aren't as doomed as our grandmothers believed. Instead of getting hung up about particular vegetables, try to get her to eat five portions of fruits or vegetables a day. This needn't be as daunting as it sounds, especially if you count up to one glass of fruit juice each day as a portion, and offer a range of different colored fruits and veggies. Many pre-teens like cherry tomatoes, peppers, and sweet potato, or sneak some mashed parsnip into creamed potatoes and chives. Baby leeks, sugar snap peas, and baby peas are three green vegetables she could try. If you really get stuck, sneak some pureed vegetables into a chicken casserole.*

23

Listen and learn

Getting pre-teens to listen to you doesn't have to mean shouting until your throat is sore. Try a couple of tricks and you'll be surprised how easily you and your children communicate.

When was the last time you listened to your children? Think you've been there, heard it all before? Know what makes your kids tick? Understand their passions, fears, and dreams?

Confident they'll come to you when they're in big trouble? For those in the know, listening skills can prevent misunderstandings, encourage children to confide in you, promote mutual respect and trust. One other big plus of really listening to your pre-teens is that they get in on the act and learn to listen to you. Is listening a dying art? Who, we wonder, is listening to all those people jabbering away on cell phones? Is it a skill that can be taught? We think so. Here's how.

SHUT UP AND LISTEN

Listening—giving someone your undivided attention—is harder to do than actually talking. In babies and small children, language arrives organically, abstract sounds slowly turning into the names of everyday objects and familiar faces. You can help

Here's an idea for you...

If your children interrupt you reading this book, don't pretend to listen, only giving them half your attention. Instead, say "I'm just in the middle of something important, but if you come back in five minutes, I'll have the time to really listen to you." If you pretend to listen, children soon realize it and pay you back when it's their turn.

by repeating the attempted word correctly until your baby or toddler has got it. Babies who don't feel heard stop trying after a while. Next comes the gradual arrival of infantile grammar. If you can, allow small children time to finish sentences. We know it is tempting to jump in when you're sure of what they are going to say, but in the long run it pays to shut up. Try to spend at least ten minutes listening to each child every day, rather than putting it off until there's a crisis.

DISTRACTIONS

You'll only be able to listen to your child if you can give her all your attention. It helps to exclude external interference by turning off the TV and radio, and turning away from the computer. You will not be able to hear properly if you are still smarting from problems at work, processing the news, worrying about what to cook or wear, and the 101 other things we use our brains for. It's also harder to hear when you are angry, sulking, agitated, or clinically depressed. If you find a way of keeping all these things at bay, please let us know and we'll be delighted to co-write a self-help book with you. Sometimes it helps to remove your child if you need to have an important conversation by taking them on a walk or somewhere away from the domestic hubbub.

Defining idea...

Arthur: "It's at times like this I wish I'd listened to my mother."
Ford: "Why, what did she say?"
Arthur: "I don't know, I never listened."
DOUGLAS ADAMS, *The Hitchhikers' Guide to the Galaxy*

BUT HOW?

By physically and psychologically meeting the kids on their turf. At a friend's funeral, the minister said he was "the sort of person to get down on the carpet with his grandchildren." You needn't wait till you become a grandparent. Being at their level helps you see and hear the world through kids' eyes and ears. Children are more receptive and more willing to share. Whatever else you remember from previous conversations, knowing the names of your children's best friends has to be one of your top priorities.

LISTENING BETWEEN THE LINES

We learn a lot about children by observing body language. You probably know that agitation, sadness, and hurt are usually expressed non-verbally, well before the words arrive. Pre-teens read your body language, too, so look at your child when you speak to her. Even toddlers recognize that still eyes mean they have Mom's undivided attention. Sit or crouch down by her, unfold your arms, uncross your legs, lean back, and smile.

LISTENING TO OLDER CHILDREN

Sometimes children, and adults for that matter, say things that seem ridiculous. They may be trying something out and their linguistic ability lags behind an idea or

If you're up for IDEA 10, *A book at bedtime*, build in time to listen to your children telling you what each story is all about.

Try another idea...

"Dr. Paula Menyuk and her co-workers found that parents who supplied babies with a steady stream of information were not necessarily helpful. Rather, early, rich language skills were more likely to develop when parents provided lots of opportunities for their infants and toddlers to 'talk' and when parents listened and responded to their babies' communications."
JANE E. BRODY, *New York Times'* personal health columnist

Defining idea...

111

thought. Time and patience help, rather than a curt rejoinder like "I don't know what you talking about." Ideas sometimes come out backwards to front and good listeners help to turn them around. If you're not sure what your daughter means, repeat back in your own words what she has said. It gives her a chance to correct you or confirm you are right. Asking questions also encourages children to tell you more. Children's dreams and aspirations might seem outlandish, but listen sincerely unless you want them to stop thinking big.

DON'TS

Don't use the word "don't." Avoid shouting from upstairs or from another room, criticizing, snapping, hectoring, nagging, giving a lecture, and repeating yourself. Generations of parents have tried these, but none of them work.

How did it go?

Q **I find it really difficult to stay interested in the stuff my kids go on about. It's the same things all the time. It's OK in small doses but when I have them all day, they drive me up the wall.**

A *Sounds like they are trying to engage you and failing miserably. Unless you attempt to take an interest in things that make them buzz, they won't feel interesting and will rant on to get a reaction.*

Q **My three-year-old notices when I am not listening to her.**

A *At least she cares enough to point this out and is not intimidated to tell you. Apologize but don't make excuses, however reasonable. Ask her to repeat herself, but this time giving her your undivided attention.*

24

Nobody likes me

Left off a guest list or never invited to a tea party? What to do when she says, "Nobody likes me."

Friendships are important. They teach pre-teens to cooperate, share, solve problems, and see things from another person's point of view. The types of friendships pre-teens make have lasting effects on their relationships and emotional well-being in future.

Pre-teens who aren't able to make or keep friends are more likely to drop out of school, play hooky, or become depressed in their teens.

If your pre-teen is getting despondent about her inability to make or keep friends, it may be that she lacks the confidence and social skills successful children have. It's worth spending time practicing different ways of saying hello, how to approach a group, and inviting other children to play. Role-play can be a useful way to help her experiment and find new ways of approaching others. Identify specific children she'd like to know better and ask her what they're interested in. Help her form

Here's an idea for you...

Watch your pre-teen on the playground. Children who tease others, push them around, or play roughly with them end up being rejected. Aggressive pre-teens have often learned that being a bully helps them get their own way, for instance having the swing to himself when he pushes other children off. But in the long term, other kids avoid him.

Defining idea...

"Grown-ups love figures. When you tell them you have made a new friend they never ask you any questions about essential matters. They never say to you, 'What does his voice sound like? What games does he love best? Does he collect butterflies?' Instead they demand, 'How old is he? How many brothers has he? How much does he weigh? How much money does his father make?' Only from these figures do they think they have learned anything about him."
ANTOINE DE SAINT EXUPÉRY,
The Little Prince

opening questions based on these subjects. Once she's practiced on you, she can try it for real. Console or congratulate according to what happens.

Shy pre-teens may avoid looking people in the eye or smiling at them. Ask your kids how they feel when someone smiles at them. Encourage them to smile at people they would like to be friends with and see what happens.

Teach your pre-teen the true meaning of turn taking. While most kids understand that it means "giving everyone a chance," they sometimes need more detailed explanations like: "Everyone has a turn, one by one, going around in a circle."

Alice, seven, complained that nobody wanted to play with her. Her mom spoke to the lunch lady who told her that other children found Alice bossy and she was always ordering them around. Alice's mom gently suggested that Alice ask other girls what they wanted to do at playtime. It's only a beginning, but Alice is learning the value of give and take and that other kids have good ideas as well.

Sometimes pre-teens need to be helped to face the sad truth that not everyone can be your friend, friendship is a two-way process and if someone really doesn't want to be your friend, then there's little you can do about it. It helps pre-teens if you are able to cite examples of people who have rejected your friendship in the past. Hopefully these experiences haven't destroyed you and you've lived to tell the tale.

As far as we're concerned, the sooner your pre-teen learns the difference between open and closed questions the better. If you put together a list of both groups, engage your kids using both sets. Then, suggest they come up with their own examples. In the process, they will discover how much easier it is to make friends by asking questions like: "How do you play quidditch?" or "What sorts of things do you like doing?" and how closed questions like: "What's your favorite color?" or "Do you have a pet snake?" bring conversations to a shuddering halt.

Some children lose friends at an alarming rate because they haven't learned to take turns or are sore losers. Perfect turn taking takes practice. Why not play some generation games (see IDEA 15)?

Try another idea...

Pre-teens who find it difficult to make friendships based on social chitchat often have more success with activity based relationships. Be a good sport. Refer to IDEA 23. *This sporting life.*

Try another idea...

"Each friend represents a world in us, a world possibly not born until they arrive and it is only by meeting that a new world is born."
ANAÏS NIN

Defining idea...

115

How did it go? **Q**   **My son has many arguments with his best friend. How can we help them get along better?**

A   *Listen to how he feels about these arguments without feeling you have to figure it all out for him. Arguments between children, as long as they don't escalate into physical violence or bullying, are usually best left between children. Telling your son you know he and his friend will sort things out and remaining interested in tales of reconciliation will help him learn to solve disagreements.*

Q   **Our son has diabetes and feels different from the other children in his class. He wants to fit in but feels nobody understands him. How can we help him make friends?**

A   *Help him turn what he perceives as a disability into a strength. Can he do a school project or talk on diabetes, and show off his knowledge about the pancreas or nutrition? Get him to practice using his insulin in public places away from school so he feels even less self-conscious in front of friends. It would probably help him if he knew other children with diabetes and we suggest you contact other families through a national or local diabetes society. Many organize weekends away or summer camps, where he'll find out how others manage.*

25

This sporting life

Whether they're playing soccer for the state or straggling in the school wheelbarrow race, help your pre-teen be a good sport.

Sports: pain, pleasure, or passion? Sporty pre-teens are better at taking turns, make friends more easily, learn how to take risks, are more agile, and have fewer mood swings than their non-sporty contemporaries. And if you're lucky, sports get pre-teens off your hands a couple of evenings a week and perhaps a big chunk of weekends as well.

Your attitude to your pre-teens' desire to join a soccer team or athletics club, or nagging you for a judo suit, is likely to depend on whether you love or hate such activities. But even if you hate everything to do with competitive sports you might just concede that getting pre-teens to run around with other kids is much better than letting them rot in front of the TV for hours.

Here's an idea for you...

Some activity vacations have sampler courses for pre-teens. One we knew of had twenty different things to do over a five-day period. The list included ten different sports: archery, judo, fencing, and so forth. Long enough to give them a taste but not long enough to bore them. Maybe they could find something they really excel at.

There's a ton of evidence that the current generation of young people is less fit than the previous generation and the incidence of childhood obesity is rising all the time. Team sports encourage kids to work together and teach them how to cope with success and setbacks. If your kids hate or are just loosy at ball games the array of different sports available in most urban areas is truly staggering. Fencing, sailing, canoeing, and orienteering—you name it, clubs are keen to get them young and sometimes these alternative sports are more suitable for children who prefer individual rather than a team sport. You never know, one of these might fit your pre-teen like a glove.

Organized sports, away from school, provide opportunities to make a range of new activity-based relationships. This could be a real boost if bullys in his class are picking on your child. This mutual activity often provides a basis for lasting friendships, especially useful for children who are shy or diffident in purely social settings. Marc and Toni's sons' lives have been transformed since they took up running: track in the summer and cross-country in the winter. "We had never been to one of these meets before," Toni told us, "but we're really getting into it and enjoying it. Laurie and Paul run for their under-13 and under-15 teams and Paul has already represented his county at cross-country. We've made some nice friends with other parents and we share the driving to away meets." Marc now wishes he'd taken up running when he was young.

WHERE TO START LOOKING?

We suggest you start your search in your local library. Medium and larger libraries have computer databases containing information on every sport you've heard of, and maybe some you haven't, that are available in your area. You could ask other parents, schoolteachers, or older kids.

BUT ISN'T IT HARMFUL?

Some parents—generally ones that hated sports when young—often wish to protect their offspring from this perceived trauma. Life is unfair. Some children are better coordinated, able to move faster, and are stronger. Others have less natural talent yet learn that hard work can make up the difference and realize that team's and individual's sporting activities need a mixture of talents and qualities to function properly. There will always be a small minority of children who'd far rather be making daisy chains or painting their nails. Leave 'em to it. The rest usually have lots of energy to burn and, when physically tired, will sleep better.

So little Quentin hates football? Never mind; have a look at IDEA 48, *Arty facts*. There might be something up his alley there.

Try another idea...

"Sooner or later in sport we run into situations that are too big for us to master. In real life...we can play hide and seek with reality, never facing the truth about ourselves. In sport we cannot...As a result, sport leads to the most remarkable self-discovery of our limitations as well as of our abilities."
SIR ROGER BANNISTER

Defining idea...

SWIMMING

Teaching your children to swim when they are young could save their lives. Most schools teach swimming but if they have already been taught by their parents they'll have a head start on other children who haven't been so fortunate. Being taught one on one by a parent is a much kinder way of learning than in a group. There are lots of watersports for those who don't mind getting wet, and in time your pre-teens might develop a taste for scuba diving.

How did it go?

Q I'm sorry, I hate sports: always have, always will. Unfortunately, my enlightened views are not shared by my offspring. I can't get out of going to their football games. The school I went to had hockey and baseball—and I haven't got a clue what's going on. Any tips?

A *Don't worry, most parents watching their kids playing football haven't got a clue, either. If you just study the rulebook and quietly quote it from time to time you might gain a little street cred. But you're likely to gain heaps by not making a fool of yourself like most of the other moms and dads.*

26

It's not my turn

We've seen many parents become children's unpaid cleaners, personal assistants, couriers, taxi drivers, cooks, and chambermaids. Sound familiar? Feel that there's nothing you can do? We'll help you. And make your children nicer, more interesting, and more independent in the process.

Start them early. We know a mom who said "He's too young to do chores." As her son got older, he was too busy, then too disinterested, and finally too spoiled. He's twenty-two now and has just moved back home after college. Nobody wanted to live with a slob who never cleaned up, so he went back to Mom.

A LIST TO BLITZ

The best way to get jobs done is to ask children to come up with a list of what needs doing. If they're involved, they won't see it as something you've imposed. We've included a guide of what children can do at different ages, but it's just a starting point.

Here's an idea for you...

Try household haggling. A job children want you to do is contingent on a job they need to do. For example, next time your son asks you to drive him to football practice, negotiate. Try saying "Yes, I'll drive you as soon as you give the guinea pig some food and water." Avoid nagging or reminding, and stick to your agreement. If he dawdles and is late for football practice, he's learned an important lesson about responsibility.

Defining idea...

"Strange new problems are being reported in the growing generations of children whose mothers were always there, driving them around, helping them with their homework; an inability to endure pain or discipline or pursue any self-sustained goal of any sort, a devastating boredom with life."
BETTY FRIEDAN, author and spokesperson for women's rights (mother of three)

Age	Job
2	Pick toys up off the floor
3	Help set table
4	Help put groceries away
5	Put out food and water for pets
6	Make bed
7	Water plants
8	Sew on buttons
9	Clean sink, bath, and toilet
10	Unload laundry and hang up washing
11	Make packed lunch
12	Cook basic meals

If you can get children to choose jobs, great. Don't worry if they choose things they can't do on their own. Do them together and delegate manageable activities. A useful rule is to triple the amount of time the task would take you and allow that much time initially. Praise every attempt, as this makes pre-teens confident, faster, and more accurate.

MONEY SPINNERS

When children do chores, reward them. Money works as a treat. Before you throw your hands up in horror, think about the alternative: Giving children pocket money every week and working as their slave. We suggest giving children weekly wages with a receipt of what they have earned for which jobs. This is a powerful reinforcer and also teaches them where there's room for improvements. This is, after all, how the rest of the world works.

BEDROOM BATTLE ZONES

Most bedroom battles can be figured out by sticking to two principles:

- Don't tidy them for your children
- Set specific goals

One of the things we've found out from talking to pre-teens embroiled in bedroom standoffs is that they don't know how to clean their rooms. They're clueless. So instead of yelling "Clean your room," you need to spell it out like this, "Take your clothes off the floor. Then put clean ones back in the dresser and dirty ones in the laundry basket." The first time they clean their own bedroom, break it into small tasks, like "Why don't you put all the pens in your pencil case and then put toys in your toy bag?" Break any job into small, manageable chunks and offer a reward and you need never nag again.

If you use money as your only reward, you'll soon be looking to remortgage the house. For other incentives, look at IDEA 17, *Treats*.

Try another idea...

"Where parents do too much for their children, the children will not do much for themselves."
ELBERT HUBBARD (father of four)

Defining idea...

"The secret of happiness is not in doing what one likes, but in liking what one does."
JAMES BARRIE, novelist and dramatist, author of *Peter Pan*

Defining idea...

How did
it go?

Q **Every evening I end up telling my daughter hundreds of times to clear the table. She doesn't until I shout. I hate shouting. What else can I do?**

A *Just tell her once. Sit next to her, look her in the eye, and say, "I'd like you to clear the table." Don't remind her; just leave her to it. If she doesn't clear the table, don't do any more for her until she has. So if she asks you for help with homework, say calmly, "I'll help you as soon as you've finished clearing the table." If you shout, she'll learn she only has to respond when your voice is over ninety decibels. That can be exciting for children and they end up only doing things when you holler.*

Q **My wife doesn't think I should make our children do the dishes. She says they will have enough to do when they are older.**

A *It's difficult when parents disagree, as children notice and use it to their advantage. It sounds as if your wife thinks doing all the cleaning up is a loving act. We've seen other parents learn the hard way that love doesn't mean doing everything for children: it's helping them do more for themselves. Have a look at Idea 19, Singing from the same song sheet.*

27

Let's talk about sex

How will the baby get out? What does "gay" mean? Can Daddy get pregnant? It's time to stop sidestepping the tough stuff and learn to answer your kid's colorful, curious questions.

Most pre-teens' sex education still comes from a poorly informed playground peer group.

Instead of the traditional talk about the birds and bees, or leaflets telling them to "just say no," ongoing conversations about sex prepare pre-teens for their teens, when they'll need to know but may be too self-conscious to ask questions they're now brazen about. Educating pre-teens also helps protect them against exploitation and abuse.

Just the thought of talking to pre-teens about sex makes most parents cringe. As with sex itself, there's no one right way to do it. We know it sounds topsy-turvy, but talking to pre-teens about sex doesn't make them more likely to experiment, become pregnant at fourteen, or become a promiscuous single parent. Pre-teens who know their penis from their elbow make better, safer choices. But keep it simple. Details confuse. If you feel shy or uncomfortable, try admitting it. Pre-teens will appreciate you saying something like, "I feel a bit embarrassed because it's personal so I'm not used to talking about it."

Here's an idea for you... **Why not hire or buy a sex education DVD or video and, having watched it with your pre-teens, use it as the basis for a family discussion on the issues raised?**

GETTING DOWN TO THE NITTY-GRITTY

OK, you've told them you're embarrassed, then what? Sex described without concepts like consent, closeness, commitment, warmth, respect for your partner sounds crude and mechanical. If you truly believe, however, that the best sex is enjoyed by couples in a kind, caring relationship and it is the ultimate way they can express themselves and their feelings to the other, then say so. You can also tell them that such thoughts and feelings tend to be kept secret between couples as they are private and nobody else's business.

Biological terms like vagina, penis, and copulation are useful and ensure the tone of the discussion remains serious. It is worth establishing that pre-teens understand these terms and they are cross-referenced to words in the language they already know. This may produce incongruous giggles or helpless laughter but this need not be a problem. Euphemisms are not helpful and need to be explained.

Here are our suggestions for tackling frequently asked questions:

Defining idea...

"I'm not young enough to know everything."
OSCAR WILDE

How are babies made?

Mommies have lots of little eggs in their tummies. Daddies' bodies make millions of tiny sperm. Sometimes Mommy and Daddy have a special grown-up cuddle, the closest two grown-ups can ever get, and this is called sex. In sex, a daddy puts his penis inside Mommy's vagina, sperm come out, and if they meet an egg, they can join together to make a baby.

Pre-teen struggling with peer pressure? There are lots of ways to say no. Find out more in IDEA 33, *Beating the bullies*.

Try another idea…

What is masturbation?

Masturbation is when someone rubs their penis or vagina because it feels nice. If people want to do it, they need to do it in private. People who don't want to do it are normal, too. Nobody should ever make anyone masturbate.

What is a period?

Once girls have grown up, they bleed from their vaginas for about five days each month. This happens because women's bodies need to clean out the lining of the womb, because that month a sperm didn't fuse with an egg to make a baby.

"Oh what a tangled web do parents weave,
When they think their children are naïve."
OGDEN NASH

Defining idea…

Uncle Trevor says he's gay. What's gay?

Most men fall in love with women and most women fall in love with men. However, some men fall in love with other men and some women fall in love with other women. People who fall in love with someone of the same sex are gay.

You get the idea. The best answers tend to be ones that are in your own words, using your family's language for sexual organs and bodily functions. When pre-teens are older, you may feel comfortable introducing the idea that babies are sometimes made during sex, but that grown-ups also have sex at other times to show love and feel close.

Q **My daughter asks me questions about sex but uses street slang. I don't like her using vulgar language. Any suggestions?**

A *We suggest you answer her questions and offer her some more appropriate language afterward.*

Q **I was sexually abused by an uncle when I was young and want to make sure it doesn't happen to my kids. I don't want to frighten them. What can I say?**

A *Your story is, sadly, a very common one. Nobody likes to imagine children being abused, but when it does happen, it is often done by a family friend or relative. When you talk to kids about bullying (see Idea 33, Beating the bullies), tell them that some grown-ups bully children by pretending to be their friends and then trying to touch them in a sexual way. Explain that children must never keep this secret. Look at Idea 39, Street-smart, for more on secrets and keeping kids safe.*

28

All creatures grate and smell

Lizard or llama, parrot or Pekinese, gecko or gerbil, pre-teens who care for pets learn important life lessons about love, loyalty, affection, reproduction, babies, comfort, illness, responsibility, trust, accidents, death, and grief.

All creatures grate and smell, we know. Yet for pre-teens, the therapeutic benefits of pet ownership more than outweigh the cost needed to care for them.

Pre-teen pet owners have many advantages, including better non-verbal communication, increased compassion, and even less time off school. Looking after a pet builds self-esteem and confidence. It doesn't matter if it's a frog or a dog, pet-owning kids get increased independence that helps them grow into mature, responsible teens. Little children often talk to pets and confide secrets. Having a non-judgmental listener helps kids build trusting relationships with humans.

Here's an idea for you...

You're never too young (or old) for a wormery. Wormeries are traditionally made in a glass aquarium, but any shallow, transparent container will do. There are two main types of worm: earthworms, which your pre-teen will find by digging in the garden, or tiger worms, which live in compost or manure. It's important not to mix these two types in one wormery. Layer sand and soil alternately in the container. Top with a few leaves and add the worms that your little hunter-gatherer has found. All your children need to do is keep the soil damp, and in return watch worms worming their way through the layers, leaving casts on top. As long as you add some new leaves, the wormery will keep going (though it gets boring once all the layers have mixed).

IT'S AN AGE THING

Pre-school kids are too young to have sole responsibility for a pet. They'll need your help and reminders to put out food and water. But once children are seven or eight, they're usually old enough to take the bulk of the responsibility.

Rodent or reptile?

When helping your pre-teen choose a pet, get them to list what they are looking for. Susie wanted to breed pets, so her dad put some tadpoles in the pond. Every year, the frogs return to breed. Ollie wanted company after school and is enjoying training Wendy, his parrot, to talk. Jose was looking for comfort after his mom died so his dad bought him a cuddly chinchilla. The Goldfrapp family can't imagine life without Caspar, their loyal Labrador. Of course, it's also important to think about practicalities. While nobody living in a one-bedroom apartment with triplets would buy a Great Dane, even a tiny hamster can be troublesome. Hamster Fudge kept the whole Kennedy family awake with endless laps on his wheel. During the day when the children wanted to play with him, he slept and grumpily nipped their fingers when they woke him. The Kennedys didn't realize hamsters were nocturnal, or that theirs would spend his nights training for a marathon.

"The dog was created specially for children. He is a god of frolic."
HENRY WARD BEECHER, Presbyterian minister

Defining idea...

Something fishy

Fish make fantastic first pre-teen pets. It's easy for children to sprinkle food into a tank and watch, then take over cleaning out the tank. It's also possible to leave fish over a long weekend with a special food block. Pre-teens can learn discipline, patience, kindness, and attentiveness from caring for a simple goldfish.

Pocket pets

Pocket pets are small mammals like rats, mice, and hamsters. Generally cheap and cheerful, these can be good, low-maintenance pets. Most seven-year-olds can learn how to clean out their cage and they don't take up much space. We like gerbils because they are awake during the day, fairly intelligent, but best of all, their urine doesn't smell. All pocket pets are talented escape artists and dedicated chewers, so we suggest you don't keep them in the same room as computer cables.

"Animals are such agreeable friends—they ask no questions, they pass no criticisms."
GEORGE ELIOT, *Scenes of Clerical Life*

Defining idea...

131

Defining idea...

"Pet ownership was significantly associated with better school attendance rates. This was apparent across all classes, but was most pronounced in the lower school (classes one to three, age groups five to eight). Here, the pet owners benefited from up to eighteen extra half-days schooling per annum than their non-pet owning counterparts."
DR. JUNE MCNICHOLAS, health psychologist

It's a dog's life

With over 350 breeds to choose from, there will be a breed for most pre-teens, if not every parent's budget. Adult dogs from rescue homes sound like a good idea, but often have lots of behavior problems and are less tolerant and snappier toward young pre-teens. Puppies are your best bet. Kids can be involved in training them and feel a greater sense of ownership. And just think of the photo opportunities. Seriously, though, a dog is for life, so it might be worth looking after a friend's dog while she's on vacation to see if your kid's interest is a fad or the real thing.

Feeling catty

Older cats tend to behave around pre-teens. They walk off if they don't like the noise and if they can't stand the children, they'll move in with the infertile couple down the road.

Kittens are unpredictable, friendly, and playful one minute, snarly and swiping the next. Great training for when you have a house full of teenagers.

Snakes, spiders, and other creepy crawlies

Forget the stereotype. It isn't just earnest, bespectacled boys who look after giant snails and scorpions. If you're squeamish, look on the bright side. Nothing will get you over arachnophobia faster than finding an escaped tarantula in your bathtub. Before handing over the money for an exotic pet, there's one thing you need to know: How big does it get? Tristan's dinky iguana grew to over one and a half feet in two years.

It's not just pets that that can teach your children about responsibilty and nurturing. Looking after plants can do this, too. Check out IDEA 32, *How does your garden grow?*, for some ideas for budding gardeners.

Try another idea...

PET HATES

Some children get bored with pets once the novelty wears off. Being older and generally more responsible, parents feel lumbered with the day-to-day chores of animal husbandry. Try not to get involved at the early novelty stage, so good habits are instilled in your pre-teens. Become a supervisor rather than a coworker.

How did
it go?

Q   My sons pestered us for a puppy. Now that Fido is bigger, they've lost interest in walking him and often forget to put food out. What can I do?

A   When you take on a pet, it becomes a member of the family. Maybe your children were too young, and thought of the puppy like a stuffed animal. If your pre-teens aren't able (or willing) to look after Fido, unfortunately, it's up to you. Instead of making Fido's care a tiresome chore, turn it into a treat. "Let" the boys walk Fido as a reward for good behavior. Or try "You won't be able to feed Fido this morning, because you're not ready for school yet."

Q   My daughter is five. She wants her own pet, but I'm not keen on cleaning out a fish tank every week. Where else can she start?

A   A stick insect is easy to look after. She can keep them in an old coffee jar with a few bramble shoots. All she needs to do is spray the bramble with water every day and change the bramble when it wilts.

29

Order, order

If meetings are the bane of your life, introducing them at home might seem perverse. We'll show you ways of keeping office politics at the office, while you and your family sort out domestic disputes democratically.

Well-conducted family meetings have many virtues: a forum for open and honest debate, a chance for grievances to be aired and heard, and opportunities to introduce a democratic element into family life.

By exploring one child's difficulties, you'll see how your family is interdependent and you affect each other. Your pre-teens can use these occasions to learn skills like chairing meetings or arguing a case for something they feel passionate about, which will prove invaluable in later life. Some parents we've met worry that group pressures might undermine their authority. You will always be the first among unequals. If your reasoning is sound and well argued, your kids are more likely to go along with your decisions rather than by blind trust.

Here's an idea for you...

Distractions play havoc with meetings. Switch on the answering machine and turn cell phones off. Make enough drinks and snacks to get everyone through the meeting—no wandering off for refills.

GETTING STARTED

Try to find positive things to put early in the agenda: a discussion where the next vacation should be, alternatives to the Sunday roast, or suggestions for family outings to a film. Some suggestions will be unrealistic ("Let's go to Disneyland!") but still deserve a considered response from you. Even off-the-wall remarks may contain elements that can be worked with and a compromise found.

MAKE A DATE

Find a suitable time and place to hold meetings. We've found that where meetings are only held at times of crisis, conflict rather than support occurs. It helps to establish a list of realistic ground rules that everyone can agree and stick to. Mutual respect, only one person allowed to speak at once, no complaining outside the meeting, a pledge to stick to the meeting's time limits, and a willingness to go with agreed outcomes are a few to begin with. You might experiment by using an egg timer to prevent someone from speaking too long or passing an object to the speaker that he or she holds while speaking to prevent interruption. Timing is everything: too long and everyone gets bored and frustrated; too short and only the assertive and loud get heard. Aim for forty-five minutes once a month at a time that doesn't clash with anyone's activity.

ROLE REVERSAL

Effective meetings tend to be those conducted with agreed roles, a chair, and someone else to record outcomes. While initially you will hold these positions, we'd encourage you to share them as soon as possible. Apart from steering the meeting through the agenda, the chairperson is responsible for ensuring everyone is heard. This means encouraging quieter members of your family to speak up and verbose members to step back and listen.

Everyone shouting over everyone else? If this is happening at your meetings, look at IDEA 23, *Listen and learn*, for ways of breaking the deadlock.

Try another idea...

FAMILY AFFAIRS

Meetings take on a life of their own, reflecting the input of everyone there. While it is important to ensure that these sessions are used to plan fun activities, more serious issues can be raised and resolved. Meetings can be used for everything from resolving domestic squabbles—no one else bothers to wash up—to expressing concern about another family member showing signs of stress. The expertise and brainpower of the collective family can be used to find solutions or, when there is no answer, empathize with this person's plight.

"Honest disagreement is often a good sign of progress."
MAHATMA GANDHI, who believed children learn better from families than from schools

Defining idea...

How did it go?

Q **Much as I'd love to have family meetings, I'm too busy and anyway my working day is full of them and I need a break.**

A *Prefer to wait for a crisis and respond by throwing a bunch of time at it? Well-conducted family meetings needn't take long and could save you hours in the long run.*

Q **We have been holding meetings for a while now and seem to have gotten bogged down in the same issue. What can we do?**

A *Why not have a brainstorming session where everyone suggests solutions? There won't be one that suits everyone, but choose the one everyone least objects to and try it out for a month. Resolve not to discuss it at future meetings until the trial period is over.*

Q **Our family meetings go on for too long, and seem to linger on informally in the rest of the house for ages afterward. Please advise.**

A *Why not set the meeting for forty-five minutes before a family meal or trip to the movies? Recording outstanding issues that need further airing at the next meeting helps, too.*

30

The best days of their lives

You can't guarantee your pre-teen's school days will be the best days of his life, but choose the right school and you can be certain he'll have many invigorating, exhilarating, and inspiring days there.

Different families have different priorities and expectations for pre-teen education. It's worth making a list of what's important and keeping it by you as you study prospective schools.

Visit as many as you can. One of the hardest, but most important, things to do is get a sense of the atmosphere and ethos. Does the place shout "discipline" or leave you feeling inspired and positive? What do you think of the cultural and ethnic diversity? Is there evidence of pre-teens' proficiency and teachers' passion for making hard tasks (like long division) achievable? Some schools ooze creative cool. But whips and chains in a principal's office are never a good omen.

Is there a school choir? Can anyone join? It won't do much for your singing six-year-old's self-esteem if she's rejected. Look out for extracurricular activities: art, band, orchestra, sports teams, plays, and productions. Where have all the school buses gone? How will your pre-teens get to school? Are there good public transportation links or will you have to drive them?

Defining idea...

"Suppose Mozart had not been allowed to begin his music until the other children did, or to practice or progress faster, or had only the instruction of a school class in music... Suppose he had been kept from playing with older children or adults in the fear that he might become socially maladjusted...kept from public performance because that would have been exploiting the child! It surely may be questioned whether he would have reached the prominence he did. Abuses in the aforementioned directions are, of course, possible. But it is also an abuse to withhold opportunities from precocious youngsters who are eager to advance and excel."

SIDNEY L. PRESSEY, educational psychologist

Schools are often keen to show off a sheaf of paper promises and policies, but dig deeper. Rather than just looking at their anti-bullying policy, ask them when it was last used successfully. When you meet the class teacher, ask yourself if you could get along with her and if you can imagine your pre-teen enjoying learning from her. Ask the principal what the school's greatest achievement is and what challenges her school is facing. If she squirms, it's time to make your excuses and leave.

FIRST DAY OF SCHOOL

There's no doubt about it. Kids who've been to nursery or pre-school will have an easier first day, perhaps even first term, than pre-teens who stayed at home. Nursery graduates are used to being separated from parents and know they'll see you again at the end of the school day. They're also used to being with other children and are better able to share and work together. Pre-teens who missed out on nursery school may not trust you will come back for them.

WHEN THINGS GO WRONG

Without being too intrusive, you can keep an eye on pre-teens' school progress. Does she seem to be enjoying school? Coping with the work? Making friends? If there are problems in any of these areas, we suggest you make an early appointment to see her teacher. Getting involved while problems are still small is far preferable to watching and waiting. When you meet the teacher, bear in mind that offering solutions will help your pre-teen more than stating problems.

MOVING TO SECONDARY SCHOOL

Moving from the one-class, one-teacher setup to a big campus with many teachers and different classrooms can be a massive culture shock for many pre-teens. Uprooted from a nurturing environment, they frequently flounder in one that seems more competitive. Give them a feel and flavor by arranging to visit their secondary school before they start there, and listen to worries they may have. Many will miss friends who are going elsewhere. Inviting them over to swap "new school" stories can make these separations less traumatic.

A HEAD START

Whatever school your pre-teen attends, your relationship with his class teacher or principal will have a big impact on his life in school. What you need to avoid is the common scenario where

Here's an idea for you...

Join the parent-teacher association. You'll have a bigger say in what happens at your child's school, and more chances to meet the teachers. Why not go the whole way and become a PTA chairperson? You'll have easy access to the principal and a useful addition to your résumé.

Try another idea...

Struggling to do your daughter's long division? Check out IDEA 31, *Homework heaven*.

Defining idea...

"People commonly educate their children as they build their homes, according to some plan they think beautiful, without considering whether it is suited to the purposes for which they are designed."
LADY MARY MONTAGU

parents' first contact with their child's teacher is when there's a problem. This sets the tone for future conversations and you risk being remembered in association with that problem.

How did it go?

Q **We would like our son to go to a small, highly selective secondary school that is well-known for teaching science. He is unhappy because he wants to go to the local public school to stay with his friends. How much choice should we give him?**

A *It's a difficult decision. On one hand, we understand you have his education at heart; on the other, we feel that if you ignore his protests, he might become more unhappy and withdrawn. Kids spend a large chunk of childhood in school, so it's important that he is happy there. Why not take him to visit both schools again? If he really doesn't want to go to the more selective school, we suggest you let him go to the school his friends are at and monitor his progress in science. A compromise might be that he has a weekly science tutor at home or uses a home learning science course. He won't fulfill his true potential in a school he doesn't want to be at.*

31

Homework heaven

Desperate to help your pre-teens out of the homework hell you remember from your childhood? Here's how to avoid history repeating itself.

Many pre-teens see homework as a chore, something that has to be done to stay out of trouble. We think this is a travesty of what homework should be.

At its best, education is a series of mind-broadening experiences that introduce pre-teens to subjects that become lifelong passions. Homework is an important part of that process.

HASSLE-FREE HOMEWORK

Teachers tell us homework is a means of consolidating, reinforcing, and supplementing school lessons. But there are many other potential benefits: Children who get on top of homework learn to be good time managers, become well organized and self-motivated, and have better recall. They discover the joy of leading a pack instead of always striving to catch up. They can relax on a Sunday evening, enjoying a well-deserved rest, when less organized and procrastinating playmates are anxiously trying to produce something, anything, to avoid the terrors

Here's an idea for you... **During a family meal why not get everyone to brainstorm a difficult homework question? It could open all sorts of new avenues and make what otherwise might have been a hard slog into an assignment your son or daughter will enjoy.**

Defining idea... **"Don't limit a child to your own learning, for he was born in another time."**
RABBINICAL SAYING

Defining idea... **"Never help a child with a task at which he feels he can succeed."**
DR. MARIA MONTESSORI

of missing an important deadline. The organized pre-teen has time to get to the library, do additional online research, and borrow the best books before everyone else.

TEN STEPS TO HOMEWORK HEAVEN

1. Use Grandma's rule

Call us old-fashioned but Grandma's rule, "first you work, then you play," has worked for generations. Pre-teens who get down to homework while the lesson is still recent and fresh have a big advantage over those who wait until the last minute a week later.

2. Have a dedicated homework area

Most pre-teens work best in a clutterless environment, free from distractions like toys, games, music, and TV. A few can work and even thrive amid noise and visual distractions most of us would find intolerable. If your pre-teen is happier working with a background of loud music and still comes up with the goods, so be it. Parents who impose "successful solutions" will be resented. Having said that, good lighting and comfortable seating improves everyone's concentration. It also helps if kids do their homework away from other family members who are not working.

3. Protect homework time

Create a working atmosphere by having a dedicated homework time. Each family is different. Your kids might prefer to get homework out of the way as soon as they get home; others need a break and work better

Worried about what your son is really up to when he "researches" his biology homework online? Have a look at IDEA 34, *Safe surfin'*.

Try another idea...

after dinner. You can reinforce your children's resolve by using this time to carry out your own paperwork, demonstrating good working principles. As children get older they should need less direct support but, unless you make it overpowering, your interest in their work will help spur them on.

4. Help children prioritize homework

A homework diary helps you and your kids see at a glance what needs doing and when it's due. Younger children and those who are still honing their organizational skills need a little prompting. Try asking, "What do you need to do this evening?" and guide them in the right direction.

5. Make a computer schedule

As soon as homework has been prioritized, draw up a schedule for using the computer. If it causes squabbles, delegate the schedule to the kids to figure out. Have a look at Idea 3, *Squabbling siblings*.

"Most of the important things in the world have been accomplished by people who have kept on trying when there seemed to be no help at all."
DALE CARNEGIE, author of *How to Win Friends and Influence People*

Defining idea...

6. Suggest pre-teens choose an easy piece of homework first

Choosing an easy subject first gives pre-teens a sense of mastery and motivates them to continue on.

Defining idea...

"Children have to be educated, but they have also to be left to educate themselves."

ERNEST DIMNET, *The Art of Thinking*

7. Plan breaks

You know your kids better than anyone and probably have a good idea of their concentration spans. Plan regular breaks and get them to do something physical for ten minutes, like showing off their new dance routine or football skills. A kitchen timer can be useful for timing breaks.

8. When children get stuck, ask them questions

You are not your children's teacher and it would be unrealistic to try. Learning to find solutions is an important part of pre-teen development. It's a good idea to ask children open questions like, "What information would help you?" and "Where could you find it?" rather than doing what we'd all love to do: Show off and tell them the answer.

9. Keep them on task

Concentration lapses and distractions are inevitable. Initially, children will need you to help steer them toward completing homework tasks. Some have real trouble settling down to work. If this happens, we suggest you see how your child is doing every twenty minutes. If he's abandoned his story writing and is playing with Legos instead, the trick is to focus on what he's done well and make a big deal about it. Instead of telling him off for playing, try handling it more like this: "I'm happy you've made a start by writing the title. I can't wait to hear the next part of your story when I come back in twenty minutes."

10. Try not to take over

As any parent knows, homework offers insights into what your children are being taught and it is often surprisingly interesting. Apart from new things you were never taught, the old stuff seems a lot more engaging the second time around. Learning with your kids is great, but we'll send you to the back of the class for taking over.

Q   **My eight-year-old gets stuck with things I never learned at school. How can I help?**

How did it go?

A   *Sounds like he needs a study buddy. If there is another classmate living nearby, you could encourage them to do homework together. But if he doesn't understand what is being expected of him he should be encouraged to clarify this with the teacher concerned.*

Q   **I work late so can't supervise my child's homework.**

A   *Aim to encourage rather than supervise. Take a keen interest in the end product and ask her how she got there. You could discuss what was learned in the process and how she could have done it differently. Good work that is produced at home should be acknowledged there as well as at school, in particular the trouble and effort she has made. This may not be so apparent to a teacher, who only sees the end product and not the work it took to get there. If your daughter really can't work unsupervised, get her into a study group or find a tutor.*

32

How does your garden grow?

Want to teach pre-teens about nurturing, growing, survival, and having a garden full of butterflies? If you plant together, you'll grow together. Come and smell the roses.

Gardening teaches kids where living creatures come from. Children who grow things have a greater sense of wonderment and responsibility, as they soon see plants die if they forget to water them.

WATER FOR LIFE

To teach pre-teens how plants take in water, why not fill a jam jar with water and add a few drops of red food coloring? Pick a few long stemmed daisies together and put them in the jar. As red water is sucked through the stem, it colors the daisy petals.

SEEDS OF HOPE

In our experience, it's better for kids to start with quick-growing plants, so they don't lose interest. Cress is an old favorite. But did you know kids could grow grass seed,

Here's an idea for you...

Stuck for a present? Take a homegrown plant. If your pre-teen decorates the pot (see IDEA 48, *Arty facts*) her present will be extra special. For an unusual Easter gift, your children could make an egghead. They'll need some markers to draw a face on an empty eggshell that has had its top knocked off. Fill the shell with used tea bags and sprinkle some mustard and cress seeds on top. Imagine Grandma's face when she sees the egghead's hair sprouting. Egghead hair can be styled with nail scissors: Try a Mohawk or buzz cut.

birdseed, and even guinea pig food in the same way? Just make sure that the results don't end up in the salad. Layer some wet kitchen paper or wet an old sponge. Then get your kids to write their names in seeds. Keep the sponge in a warm place and get the kids to keep it moist. In a few days' time, their names will start sprouting.

FLOWER POWER

As you know, pre-teens love color and also need rapid results. Bright, bold sunflowers grow up to 12 inches in a week. Sunflower seeds are available cheaply in pet shops and health food shops. Get your pre-teens to plant them 1 inch apart and keep the soil well watered.

Borage, or starflower, also grows quickly, and kids can cut up the leaves into a salad. The small blue flowers are edible. For a summer treat, why not freeze borage flowers into ice cubes and serve in glasses of pink lemonade. Unforgettable.

If your pre-teens' fingers are more sticky sweet than green, try growing chocolate cosmos. These stunning deep-red flowers have a delicious, heady, chocolatey smell.

HELPING HANDS

Many little ones love to "help" in the garden. Make sure you give specific instructions. Asking pre-teens to "weed the garden" almost guarantees they'll uproot your prize dahlias. Instead, try asking pre-teens to see how many daisies and buttercups they can pick out of the lawn or slugs they can collect from the lettuce plot.

Why not encourage your children to share their gardening successes (and failures) with their grandparents? IDEA 12, *Grandparents: help or hindrance?*, describes long-distance gardening.

Try another idea...

BUTTERFLY GARDEN

Pre-schoolers love butterflies. Whether they're intrigued by their beauty, grace, and gossamer wings or more interested in chasing them, making a butterfly garden with your pre-teens is one of the best ways to spend spring. If you're still not convinced, we ought to tell you butterfly gardens are fantastic places for parents to hang out. Maybe with a cocktail on a long summer evening?

There's no easy way to say this, but you need to give pre-teens the sunniest spot in your garden. Neither pre-teen gardeners nor butterflies will flourish in the barren patch in the shade by the fence. Butterflies need sunny spots for basking, places to shelter from wind and rain, and a source of fresh water. You'll need at least two muddy puddles, one for male butterflies to get salts essential for reproduction, and the other for pre-teens to make big splashes in.

You'll also need two types of plant: nectar plants for adult butterflies to eat and host plants, which caterpillars eat. Lady butterflies are good mothers. They'll only lay eggs on host plants so their baby caterpillars don't have to travel to eat. Seeing the whole butterfly life cycle is fascinating for pre-teens, so we suggest they plant both types. As you know, different plants grow on different types of soil, so your pre-teen will need to do a bit of research at the library and garden center. In some areas it's possible to attract certain species of butterfly with particular plants. Involve children in choosing, watering, weeding, and caring for their garden.

POT LUCK

Pre-teens who live in apartments needn't miss out. They can garden in containers on balconies or windowsills. Growing things to eat is fun, and it's great to show off produce at family meals and to friends. We've successfully grown so-called "patio tomatoes" on a tiny balcony, as well as sweet and chili peppers in brightly painted terra-cotta pots. We know pre-teens who grow miniature pumpkins on their windowsill. They taste great, but the real bonus is that they make fantastic lanterns for harvest or Halloween. Alternatively, once pumpkins are a couple of inches across, ask your pre-teen to draw a face or write their initials in ballpoint pen. Then go over their face or initials with a compass, using enough pressure to just break the skin. As the pumpkins grow, their faces or initials will, too.

How did it go? **Q** **Our five-year-old daughter is very interested in growing fruit from seeds. She pots them in soil, but is sad when nothing happens.**

A *Small fruit like apple, pear, orange, and lemon need to be soaked in water overnight before she plants them. We also suggest she covers the seed with about two fingers' depth of potting compost. Covering the pot in plastic wrap for a few days and keeping the compost moist should also help. If she wants to grow cherry, apricot, or nectarine from pits, crack the pit with a nutcracker before soaking.*

33

Beating the bullies

Let's not beat around the bush—bullies cannot be allowed to harm our kids. But how can you help without making things worse?

How can you tell if your children are being bullied?

Common warning signs include refusing to go to school, playing hooky, avoiding the usual route to school, irritability, coming home hungry, unexplained bruises or scratches, black moods, cruelty to brothers and sisters, unhappiness, and suicidal feelings. Any of these symptoms may have other causes, but if you notice several of them occurring together over a few weeks, it's likely your child is being bullied.

You may feel like pulverizing the bully's parents. Alternatively, you might think that playground bullying is between children and that you and other adults shouldn't get involved. Left unchecked, bullying can be disastrous for children, leading to isolation, low self-esteem, and depression. In later life they may find it hard to start and maintain trusting relationships, suffer stress-related illnesses, and misuse drugs and alcohol. You can teach your children to respond to bullies in an assertive rather than aggressive way.

Here's an idea for you... Next time you watch a cartoon or read a comic with your kids, encourage them to look at the characters' body language. It helps to turn off the volume. Get your pre-teens to list bully and victim characteristics. In Tom and Jerry cartoons, for example, most of the time Tom stands tall and menacing, while Jerry crouches and slinks around. However, when Jerry stops being a victim, he puffs out his chest, making himself look big. Encourage your children to try different body language, seeing if they can make themselves look threatening, victim-like, or assertive. Teach them to fake it till they make it.

NEW WAYS OF RESPONDING TO BULLIES

Tell your children to pick up on what the bully says but reply in a way that neutralizes an insult. For example:

"You smell."
"Yes, it's my new shampoo. It smells great."

Another ruse is to teach children to ask bullies to "say it again." As most bullies are cowards, they lack the courage to repeat an insult and are more likely to tone it down. Encourage them to keep asking the bully to repeat the insult until it is inoffensive. Teach them to imagine themselves inside a protective bubble that bounces off bullies' words. If they practice visualizing this, they will be distracted when bullies are trying to insult them. It also gives some control back to them in a potentially disempowering encounter. Make sure your children have chances to make friends away from where bullying takes place. A drama group, sports club, orchestra, or choir is ideal because they provide a shared activity that can rebuild confidence eroded by bullies.

Suggest your child keeps a diary of bullying incidents. Writing down what happened and how they feel is a helpful way of managing sadness, anger, and profound unfairness. If you date and countersign entries with your comments, this will be useful if you need to take further action. Children who are too young to write need not miss out. A collage, painting, or clay model of what has happened or how they feel can be equally cathartic. Children who feel angry and violent can feel better by making and smashing a clay model.

Encourage them to tell a teacher. If children feel they cannot do so, find out if they will tell another adult in school: lunch lady, secretary, or school nurse. Some feel unable to talk about it but are able to write down what has happened or show their diary.

If bullying is persistent, or your child is injured, take action. If bullying happens at school, take the matter up with a suitable teacher and work upward until the matter is taken seriously and addressed. Keep written records. Don't hesitate to involve the police if bullies threaten or injure your child.

Brainstorm ways to say "no." Children who have successfully said no to bullies came up with the following list:

Here's an idea for you...

- No.
- No, I don't want to.
- No thank you.
- No, I prefer not to.
- If it was up to me I would, but my mom won't let me give my things away.
- I have diabetes and that makes it dangerous for me to miss lunch.
- It's against my religion.

Once children have found and practiced ways of saying no that feel comfortable, they are better able to stand up for themselves.

Try another idea...

Children who have had a difficult day being bullied at school need a lighter atmosphere at home. Sometimes, deconstructing events and poring over minutiae is unhelpful. Diversion may be more constructive. Have fun. Play some generation games (IDEA 15).

Defining idea...

"I found one day in school a boy of medium size ill-treating a smaller boy. I expostulated but he replied: 'The bigs hit me, so I hit the babies; that's fair.' In these words he epitomized the history of the human race."
BERTRAND RUSSELL

Defining idea...

"In a prison they may torture your body; but they do not torture your brains; and they protect you against violence and outrage from your fellow prisoners. In a school you have none of these advantages."
GEORGE BERNARD SHAW

Q   **Life is tough. Isn't it better that my son learns to stand up for himself and physically fights off bullies?**

How did it go?

A   *If he learns to fight back, he learns that violence is an acceptable way of solving problems. He can stand up for himself by being assertive, but if he uses force he becomes a bully himself.*

Q   **Recently my daughter has been "losing" her lunch money. I suspect that some older girls are making her give it to them but she won't talk about it. What can I do?**

A   *Subtly slip the subject of overcoming bullying into ordinary conversations. Talk generally about bullying; for example, if you read a story together where a character is being bullied. Or talk about people like Winston Churchill, Jamie Lee Curtis, or Harrison Ford who have succeeded despite being bullied. If she hints at any trouble in school, praise her for being brave enough to tell you. Reassure her that the bullying will stop but tell her you need a bit more information so you can help her. You will find useful hints in Idea 23, Listen and learn. If she still doesn't open up, be direct. Say something like, "Some children who tell their parents they lost their lunch money are really being bullied and I am worried that may be happening to you. Let's talk about it."*

Q   **Our daughter has been bullied for months and recently I overheard her telling a friend that she sometimes feels suicidal. I don't know how to respond. Please help.**

A   *You need to take this very seriously. Sadly, a number of children have committed suicide after prolonged bullying. Tell her calmly what you overheard, get professional help, and consider withdrawing her from school.*

34

Safe surfin'

The Internet is a fantastic resource. Mostly, it's useful and fun. Understandably, parents worry about well-publicized dangers like perverts and email bullies. We'll show you how to keep kids safe from offensive, pornographic, and other frightening stuff.

Shared surfing is enjoyable and educational. We've found you can't start teaching kids computer skills too soon—most two-and-a-half-year-olds can click a mouse.

We recommend keeping Internet access on a family computer in a communal area, like a living room, rather than in children's bedrooms. Pre-teens might protest, but without wanting to scare you, we feel their protests are far preferable than being preyed on by an online pedophile. Comercially available software filters that block access to sites featuring adult material can be useful, especially if curious kids can guess your password. Many parents feel pre-teens are entitled to more privacy as they get older. We agree, as you won't always be able to supervise older kids, and especially now that Internet sites can be accessed from cell phones.

Here's an idea for you... **Set rules about how long individuals can spend on the computer, stipulating times of day when the Internet may not be used.**

Defining idea... **"Parents think their children should keep their innocence as long as possible. The world doesn't work that way."**
GRACE HECHINGER, *How to Raise a Street-Smart Child*

Defining idea... **"Permissiveness is the principle of teaching children as if they were adults, and the tactic of making sure they never reach that stage."**
HELENA PETROVNA BLAVATSKY, theosophist

SITES FOR SORE EYES

Find out which sites your pre-teens visit by integrating conversations about the Internet into offline chats. For example, when you talk about dangers outside the home, mention Internet dangers, too. Tell them about chat rooms and that sometimes people may not be who they claim to be. When it's your son's turn to choose a treat, perhaps you could buy it online and show him how Internet shopping works. Similarly, when your daughter asks questions about sex, take the opportunity to talk about pictures she might be sent on email or sites that might upset or scare her.

EASY ESSAYS

More and more children are using the Internet to help with homework. At best, this means their work is less original than classmates who use other sources. Plagiarism is becoming a big problem and many children are unaware that downloading chunks of text and passing it off as their own is a crime that in time could get them thrown out of school. Stress that other people's writing should be used as a resource, what they learn from them needs to be reworked in their own words, and anything that is quoted needs to be attributed.

BULLYING

Because emails and cell phones weren't widely available when we were growing up, it can be a shock to realize how many kids are bullied or harassed online. Remind your pre-teen to be selective about who she gives her email address to, but if she is bullied, you can provide practical support by helping her change to a new email address.

So email has messed up your pre-teen's spelling and grammar? Don't worry. Have some fun using snail mail. See IDEA 49, *Putting pen to paper*.

"The most influential of all educational factors is the conversation in a child's home."
SIR WILLIAM TEMPLE, diplomat and author

Try another idea...

Defining idea...

How did
it go?

Q   **We have software filters, yet when our daughter goes to her friends' homes not everyone seems to use them. How can I keep her from looking at adult sites?**

A   *You're right. Every home should have software filters, but not all bother. The best software filter in the world is no substitute for good advice from home, and the conversations you have together will help her make her own choices about which sites she sees.*

Q   **My son doesn't have many friends in his class and says he prefers to "meet" people online. I'm glad he's not lonely, but I do worry about the amount of time he spends in front of the computer. Am I making a fuss for nothing?**

A   *If he is making most of his friends online, his social development will suffer, particularly his listening skills. If he doesn't see eye to eye with his classmates, perhaps an afterschool activity would be the answer?*

Q   **Our daughter has shown us some offensive emails she's been sent. We're all upset and don't know how to stop them.**

A   *We suggest you report this to your Internet service provider. While they investigate, block the sender using your email program or anti-spam software.*

35

Highflyers

There's always room at the top for those with high self-esteem. Whether they're climbing trees or the corporate ladder, give your children a leg up.

Self-esteem is one of those words usually prefaced by the word "low." Pushing kids too hard and expecting standards they can never reach is a sure way to mess up how they feel about themselves.

Kids with low self-esteem have more academic and relationship problems. In later life, they're more likely to take drugs or abuse alcohol. But we're talking about raising confident, self-assured kids who do well at school, make friends easily, have higher aspirations, and are generally more successful in life.

VARIETY'S THE SPICE OF A SELF-ASSURED LIFE

It's never too early to start. Toddlers develop self-esteem when they learn to do things on their own. Making the home safe so your toddler can explore freely helps develop their independence and self-esteem. Self-esteem is strongly associated with

Here's an idea for you... **Look for opportunities to ask your pre-teen's advice. Whether she's helping to program your new cell phone, picking a shirt and tie for you to wear to work, or helping you decide what the family should eat for dinner, involving them in decisions helps her feel she has an important contribution to make and that you trust her.**

learning new skills. Praising and encouraging children builds confidence, but stretching them with new opportunities and experiences helps them shine and sparkle. As your kids get older, try to do things together that are challenging but within reach.

WHAT AM I GOOD AT?

Encourage your pre-teen to make a "what I'm good at" collage or scrapbook. Six-year-old Sara's mom started her off by giving her a poster-size piece of cardstock and sticking a photo of Sara in the middle. Sara cut and glued pictures of a golden retriever, swimming pool, pencil, and playground. She then drew herself in different poses, showing how good she is at walking the family dog, swimming without floaties, writing, and making up dance routines on the playground. The collage is pinned up on a bulletin board in her room, so it's one of the first and last things she sees each day, helping her feel great about herself, whatever the day brings.

Defining idea... *"Once you see a child's self-image begin to improve, you will see significant gains in achievement areas, but even more important, you'll see a child who is beginning to enjoy life more."*
WAYNE DYER, psychotherapist who grew up in an orphanage

Eleven-year-old Sam has a spiral notebook in which he writes his achievements. Whether it's an A in geography or another saved goal, they're all in there. He started the book three years ago when his parents were splitting up. "I felt really down and useless," he remembers, "but writing down what I'm good at helped me see it wasn't true." Sam's book had an unexpected bonus. "It's helped me do more than I thought I could. Each week I try to beat my highest weekly achievement score." When your kids are older, these collages and books can be used for career planning—exploring which jobs are related to their talents, interests, and achievements.

TIME TO TALK

Set aside some individual time each week with each child. Aim to focus on what they say, without worrying about your laundry, mother-in-law, or layoffs. If you crouch down or kneel and make eye contact with little children, you're less likely to talk down to them or use patronizing language.

PROMISES, PROMISES

"Can I have a monkey, Mom?" asked Derek for the millionth time.

"If you're good at the store we'll buy you a monkey tomorrow," said Derek's mom with her

Want to try some new stuff with your pre-teens, but stuck for ideas? See IDEA 46, *Save it for a rainy day*.

Try another idea...

Children who do regular chores have a greater sense of responsibility which boosts self-esteem. Check out IDEA 26, *It's not my turn*, for some pointers.

Try another idea...

"When I was a kid, my father told me every day, 'You're the most wonderful boy in the world and you can do anything you want to.' "
JAN HUTCHINS, radio talk-show host

Defining idea...

"The real voyage of discovery consists not in seeking new landscapes but in having new eyes."
MARCEL PROUST

Defining idea...

165

fingers crossed. Ever felt like Derek's mom? Sometimes it's tempting to make false promises for peace and quiet. But broken promises can shatter pre-teen's self-esteem, making them feel they're unimportant and worthless.

SEPARATE THE BOY FROM THE BEHAVIOR

When your child does something naughty, aim to separate him from his misdemeanor. So instead of saying something like, "You're so stupid and messy spilling soup all over Daddy's new boss," try, "What could you do differently with your next bowl of minestrone, so it doesn't end up on anybody's lap?" By separating the act from your child, you are still able to let him know what is unacceptable without him feeling humiliated.

How did it go?

Q   There are times when it feels wrong to make my son feel good. He lies, cheats, and steals, and when I catch him and tell him off, he obviously feels bad.

A   *Kids need to feel temporarily bad and guilty after being naughty. In fact, you can use these feeling to motivate him to make amends. Confessing to forging his school report or paying back the family shopping money after stealing will bring his self-esteem back up and should improve his future behavior.*

36

Stress busters

Stress is sneaky. It creeps up on kids and can cause chaos. Forget meditation and muscle relaxation. Most pre-teens need something way more imaginative. Our stress busters will keep the sneak away.

Stressed people are often the last to recognize what is happening. Kids are no exception. Just because Josh isn't complaining about finding math stressful doesn't mean he's not suffering.

If your toddler seems to be behaving differently—irritable, crying more than usual, getting nightmares, and regressing—chances are she's stressed. Likewise, if younger children are permanently tired, not sleeping, whining, and doing badly at school, they, too, may be stressed. Older children, on the other hand, may surprise you with outbursts of anger, skip school, and generally feel bad and miserable about themselves and the rest of the world.

Pre-teens who have ongoing stress are more likely to develop colds, digestive problems, headaches, and obesity. Unless kids learn to cope with stress, they're more likely to misuse drugs and alcohol in their teens and adult life and become depressed and suicidal.

Here's an idea for you... **Find a quiet place where you won't be disturbed for a few minutes and close your eyes. Cast your mind back to the time in your life you felt most deeply relaxed. Some people like to think of a vacation, but feel free to choose anywhere. Imagine yourself in that calming place now. Try to bring it to life vividly, using all your senses. What can you see, hear, taste, smell, and feel? Stay in the place for as long as it takes to feel calm. One of the great things about pre-teens is that they are better at imagining than adults. When you teach them to imagine their calming place, you're giving them an individualized, portable stress buster.**

WHAT KICKS OFF STRESS?

It could be almost anything. The death of a pet, the arrival of a new brother or sister, Dad being laid off, parental separation, moving home, changing school, the death of a grandparent, or an unresolved family argument.

WHAT HELPS?

Sound, confiding relationships with adults are enormously helpful. It doesn't matter who they are: parents, grandparents, aunts, uncles, godparents, family friends, or even teachers. Stressed kids may not know what is causing it and it is often a mixture of more than one difficulty. What helps is an active listener, prepared to ask open questions to figure out what is wrong.

Being heard and taken seriously is a stress buster.

Other stress busters:

- Breathing slowly and deeply
- Taking a long warm bath and listening to favorite music
- Exercise
- Hobbies to retreat into
- High self-esteem
- Relaxation exercises

Most relaxation exercises rely on kids tensing and relaxing groups of muscles. Not exactly what your pre-teen is going to feel comfortable doing on the school bus before a math test. We've got a relaxation technique that kids love because they can do it anywhere and nobody else can see what they're up to.

Your kids want to escape pressure by playing rugby or horse riding? Fine, but what if it's raining? Look at IDEA 46, *Save it for a rainy day*, for all-weather activities.

Try another idea...

CALMING PLACES

When our friend Janet taught her daughter Ellie how to imagine a special calming place, they made a collage of it together. Ellie imagined herself by a lake, in a green clearing close to her grandmother's house. She drew herself in the scene and cut out felt trees and shiny blue material for the lake. When the collage was finished, she imagined herself there, telling her mother how she could feel the breeze on her face, smell flowers, feel soft grass, and in her mind's eye see herself dipping her fingers into the shallow water and making ripples. Janet wrote down what Ellie described and every evening she read it back to her. Ellie practiced retreating to her calming place: "It was hard at first," she remembers, "but once you learn to do it, you can take it anywhere." A little like riding a bike.

Eleven-year-old Anton has used this relaxation trick, too. He was being bullied at school, and although the bullying had stopped, he was very stressed out in the mornings before school and didn't want to go. He imagines being by the sea, listening to the lapping of the waves and tasting the salt spray on his face. Although he

"There is no need to go to India or anywhere else to find peace. You will find that deep place of silence right in your room, your garden, or even your bathtub."
ELISABETH KUBLER-ROSS, psychiatrist and author of *On Death and Dying*

Defining idea...

169

doesn't have a dog, he imagines his uncle's Labrador is with him and that he can stroke her fur. In the distance, he hears an ice-cream truck and can smell his favorite flavor, raspberry sorbet. When he gets into school, he feels calm and ready to face the day.

Pre-teens may struggle to visualize at first. The trick is to practice when they are not feeling particularly tense, so that they can use it easily when they need a stress buster.

How did it go?

Q **My daughter looks really cranky and wound up but when I ask her what she feels stressed about, she says, "Nothing."**

A *There are two possibilities. It can be hard to know what kids are feeling and she might not feel stressed. On the other hand, she might not be able to articulate it. If she seems overwhelmingly and chronically stressed, be direct and say something like, "Something seems to have really gotten to you. Can I help?" Have a look at Idea 23,* Listen and learn, *for hints on how to listen between the lines.*

Q **You say adults should tell kids what's going on, but if I tell our kids I've been fired, won't that just stress them out?**

A *It's less stressful for pre-teens if they know basic facts. Children think everything is their fault. Reassure them.*

37

Not in our house

Who rules your roost? We're not suggesting every family needs an operational policy or mission statement, but if you want a happy household, prevention really is better than punishment.

Whether you realize it or not, every home and family has rules. Unlike school rules, they're (usually) not written on the walls and are enforced inconsistently.

The truth is that families with agreed upon rules get along better, resolve discipline problems effectively, and have happier kids who know what's expected and how they ought to behave.

NO MORE *@!#ING SWEARING, JIMMY

Setting home rules rather than rules for pre-teens is a good idea. Not only do they apply to you, too, but also to stepchildren and friends. It's easy to feel pressured to live by another family's rules when kids come to stay for the weekend. Cries of "our mom lets us do that" are usually extinguished when you explain that these aren't your rules, they're written by everyone living here, so visitors have to live by them.

Here's an idea for you...

If compulsory attendance at family meetings is a rule, it usually hurts kids more to live with decisions made in their absence than to have their pocket money docked. We suggest you say no infrequently but mean it when you do. It's worth spending time carefully considering consequences for broken rules.

Defining idea...

"A child of one can be taught not to do certain things such as touch a hot stove, turn on the gas, pull lamps off their tables by their cords, or wake mommy before noon."
JOAN RIVERS

Defining idea...

"Feelings of worth can flourish only in an atmosphere where individual differences are appreciated, mistakes are tolerated, communication is open, and rules are flexible–the kind of atmosphere that is found in a nurturing family."
VIRGINA SATIR, pioneering family therapist and educator

The key to getting the right mix of house rules is to involve the whole family. If you ask pre-teens what the rules should be, they'll usually come up with crazy suggestions like, "Ice cream for breakfast" or "No more bedtime." But ask them questions like:

■ What do you think we need to help our family get along better?
■ What upsets you?
■ What makes playing unsafe?

Amalgamate their responses with your own feelings and expectations and you'll find common wishes: no hitting, no stealing. Mark and Selina used an original take: "We made a deal with the kids," explains Mark. "We'd set two rules for them and they could make two rules for us." Mark and Selina's rules for their kids were simple: "No swearing, no fighting." Their kids were more specific: "Tell us what's happening, don't just do things. Don't blame us, help us." It turned out they were fed up with Selina shouting, "Why do you always make a mess?" She's worked hard at saying, "How can we clear this up?" and they don't swear anymore. And fighting? "We're still working on it," admits Mark.

Specific rules, tailored to your home, are the way forward. The McErlanes live in a lighthouse. To save legwork, they have baskets at the top and bottom of their long, spiral staircase where they put things that need to be taken up or downstairs. Their family rule is that anyone going upstairs takes something from the basket up with them and vice versa. Wouldn't work in a Manhattan loft, but perfect for the lighthouse family.

LESS IS MORE

It's easy for rules to become a parental wish list: no running, no shouting, no jumping, and no splashing. The problem with wish lists is that they set pre-teens up. Nobody can be a Goody Two-shoes all day, every day. A few easily understood rules work better and help you focus on priorities. What's really important? "No entering bathrooms when other people are in there" may be all your household needs.

SHARE AND SHARE ALIKE?

Younger children usually need rules about sharing toys. A good compromise may be toys kept in communal areas are shared, but toys

Stepparents, we're afraid that biological parents know best where their pre-teen is concerned. Read all about it in IDEA 40, *Wicked stepparents.*

Try another idea...

The fairest and most pain-free way to introduce new rules is to discuss them at your next family meeting. See IDEA 29, *Order, order.* Your pre-teens might not agree with every rule, but being an open, benevolent dictator is better than implementing new regimes by stealth like a fascist autocrat.

Try another idea...

"There are very few all male households around. There are no rules, no precedents. At least we were male so we could do what we wanted."
SIMON CARR, journalist who brought up two sons alone after his wife died

Defining idea...

"Civilization begins at home."
HENRY JAMES

Defining idea...

173

kept in bedrooms are personal property and pre-teens ask before touching. This rule only works if it comes with the right to say no to another child playing with your stuff. We tell kids to share, but would you let the neighbors drive your Ferrari just because they've come by for coffee?

PICK 'N' MIX

Many parents amalgamate rules from their respective childhoods. Sabina's parents found a creative middle way between her mom's more liberal German upbringing and her dad's harsher Pakistani discipline. She was brought up with explicit expectations: politeness; compassion; work first, play later; and respect elders.

How did it go?

Q **We made it a rule that the kids have to wash their hands before dinner, but they keep forgetting.**

A *Sounds like a visual reminder would help. If they're too young to read, a big picture of a tap and a hand underneath it that they can color and hang on the wall ought to prompt them.*

Q **My daughter keeps complaining about our rules, saying that all her friends' parents are more lenient.**

A *We know this one: "But Mom, everyone else is allowed to dye their hair purple, get their tongue pierced, live in a commune," or whatever. Don't feel you have to defend your decisions. As long as she lives in your house, your house rules rock. On the other hand, is it possible you are being too strict? If all the other six-year-olds are only doing a half hour of homework and she's studying for five hours a night, it may be time to rethink.*

38

Cigarettes, drugs, alcohol

Panicking about pre-teen potheads? We thought not. It's a strange and sad fact: Most eleven-year-olds are vehemently anti smoking, alcohol, and drugs, yet just three years later, between a fifth and a third of them have experimented.

Stop tomorrow's adult addicts in their tracks.

ALCOHOL

Alcohol is teenagers' favorite drug. Three reasons teens drink:

- Magazines, films, TV, and friends tell them it's cool
- It's freely available (look in your fridge)
- To cope with boredom or stress

Bring up kids who can amuse and educate themselves (Idea 46, *Save it for a rainy day*), have ways of coping with stress (Idea 36, *Stress busters*), and be upfront about the dangers of underage drinking and you're halfway there.

And the other half? If you start talking about alcohol with pre-teens, they'll be more willing to talk to you about drinking when they're teens. Talking together about movie or magazine ads and asking pre-teens how they feel about ones that

Here's an idea for you...

Look out for opportunities to talk. If you step over a homeless heroin addict when you're out shopping, talk about the choices and consequences of choosing drugs. Encourage your pre-teen to tell you how they feel about the raid on a crack house in your neighborhood. If you're in touch with your pre-teen's interests and know her friends, she'll be more likely to confide in you and there are less likely to be big surprises.

encourage drinking takes practice, but it's worth it. But, as we've said elsewhere, children are mimics. Pre-teens who see you falling into a drunken stupor after work every night are going to be unimpressed by the "no alcohol until you're thirty" lecture on their tenth birthday. Try explaining that alcohol is OK in small amounts for grown-ups, and that we like it because it tastes nice and helps us relax. Next time you have a hangover, be up front and say that when grown-ups drink too much, it makes them feel ill. Lots of pre-teens ask why they can't drink. Saying growing bodies react badly to alcohol is honest.

SMOKING

Jodie turned her son Armand (now in his twenties) off cigarettes when he was a toddler. "My brother smoked and I'd get Armand to smell his hair and afterward I'd say, 'Didn't that smell yucky?'" Jodie took other opportunities to link smoking and bad-smelling clothes, breath, and hair. When he was older, Armand recalls her "telling me how smoking left little bits of tar in your lungs and that made it hard to breathe. She said lots of people die of cancer because of all the poison in cigarettes. Our next-door neighbor died when I was about nine and I remember Mom saying his heart had stopped because all the cigarettes furred up his blood vessels." Arnand now works as a hypnotherapist, helping people quit.

DRUGS

"Why does Tara sniff talc off the table, Mommy?" Saying "just say no" just isn't enough. When they see the babysitter doing lines of coke on the coffee table, Auntie Edna popping E, or their stepmom rolling a spliff, drugs will become part of life. If they tell you things like this, try not to drop the baby. If there's an ugly scene, they're more likely to keep these stories secret in the future. Talk about what they've seen and how they feel. It helps if you put your view across clearly, too. Pre-teens can understand that drugs are chemicals that change how we think, feel, and behave. It's a good idea to warn them that drugs can be dangerous, as they affect us in different ways. Pre-teens are most likely to experiment with glue, nail-polish remover, and paint stripper. It's important to warn kids, as pre-teens die every year sniffing substances, often for the first time. Drug-taking kids have lower self-esteem, so building this up is important (see Idea 35, *Highflyers*).

If your children don't want to talk to you about drugs, perhaps their grandparents could be a source of advice. **IDEA 12, *Grandparents: help or hindrance?*, talks about the special relationship that spans the generations.**

Try another idea...

"Parents who are open, honest, responsive, and frank encourage self-esteem, balance, and fairness in their children and give them space to think, weigh up options, decide, and act responsibly. This healthy dialogue between parents and children has to begin early, from the first question."
DR. MIRIAM STOPPARD, parenting and women's health expert

Defining idea...

177

School-age children are able to learn different names of drugs and remember that you've told them heroin and cocaine are difficult to stop taking once you've tried them and that too much can kill you. Flora explained the dangers of LSD to her son Earl: "It can be fun but other times you end up in a scary dream and see things like giant beetles and you can't wake up to get away from them." George talks to his kids about cannabis: "A lot of our friends smoke weed, and what I've said to the kids is that it makes people feel happy and chilled a lot of the time, but sometimes it can make people feel scared and mess up their thinking or make it hard to remember stuff."

How did it go?

Q **I'm pretty sure that Darren, age nine, is smoking. Both my partner and I are non-smokers and we have spoken to him about the dangers. What else can we do?**

A *Firstly, you need to find out where he is getting his supply. If he's buying them from a store, report it to the police. Perhaps talking to parents of other children involved might help. Mostly, however, you'll need to keep a dialogue going with Darren stressing the dangers of smoking and why you and your partner haven't taken up this dirty habit. If it's any consolation, you are better placed to take a high moral stance on this issue than parents who smoke a pack a day.*

39

Street-smart

We live in a mad, bad world. No wonder so many parents want to keep their children indoors 24/7. But unless you show them how to survive on the street, you'll end up with a thirty-seven-year-old who can't cross the road...and that's really scary.

Watch the news and you'd think children were being kidnapped on every corner. While it isn't quite as bad as that, children do need skills to survive without you. You know that as children grow up, they need more freedom.

Children flourish and confidence soars when they're allowed to explore worlds outside their front door. But at the same time they need to cross busy roads, avoid accidents, cope when they get lost, and avoid mistreatment. The secret of raising street-smart pre-teens is a genuine desire to see them think and act for themselves.

Here's an idea for you... **Next time you go out, get your children to choose a suitable place to cross the road and tell you when it's safe to cross. As soon as they can try new ideas out in practice, they'll be reinforced and remembered. Or ask a question like, "Say you got lost here, who could you ask for help?" Try to keep your tone casual or you'll frighten them and they'll be clingy rather than independent.**

ROAD RUNNERS

Seven-year-old Luis was hit by a car when he misjudged how quickly he could cross the road. Azim didn't see his toddler playing in the drive when he reversed out of the garage. Six-year-old George ran into the road after his new kitten. Most parents and schools teach basic road safety. Despite this, many children are injured or killed by cars every day.

Children are copycats. The best way to teach road safety is by demonstration. As adults, we are better at judging distances and car speeds, so can dart across a road relatively safely. Pre-teens can't do this consistently. Instead of paying lip service to traffic safety, then running across the middle of the road with your children, cross streets at corners, use pedestrian crossings whenever you can, and make eye contact with drivers before crossing in front of their car.

FREEWHEELING

The day your child learns to ride a bike without training wheels is a major milestone on the road to independence. Suddenly, she can explore the neighborhood without Dad's taxi. But even as you watch her ride off into the sunset, most parents worry. Bikes cause more childhood injuries than anything except cars. Reducing the risk of serious head injury by up to 85 percent is simple:

a helmet. Before buying one, check it sits on top of your child's head, covering her forehead, and doesn't wobble around. Helmets aren't just for cycling. Next time your child uses his skates, scooter, or skateboard, protect his head.

Need a few tips on helping children to be more assertive and say no? Look at IDEA 33, Beating the bullies.

Try another idea…

LOST AND FOUND

Getting lost is scary. It must be a massive relief when someone helps you find Mom or Dad. And that's why children need to know who to approach. Teach them to look for the following people, in this order:

- Policeman or woman
- Security guard
- Anyone in uniform (crossing guard, postal worker, checkout assistant)
- A woman with children
- A woman without children

Before you accuse me of being sexist, children are less likely to be abducted by women, so it's a safer bet. Most parents teach children their name, address, and phone number but it is worth checking that young children also know your full names, not just "Mommy" and "Daddy."

"Perhaps we have been misguided into taking too much responsibility from our children leaving them too little room for discovery."
HELEN HAYES, actress and writer, recipient of the Jefferson Award for humanitarian work

Defining idea…

Some children never get lost. Others seem to have a talent for it. They slip between clothes racks in shops, slide past you in the park, disappear behind a tree. If you have a pre-teen like this, buy them a whistle. I know it sounds silly, but think of it like this: They're cheap, colorful, and can be blown for longer than any child can shout or cry. A word of warning: For your bedtime story (see Idea 10) read *The Boy Who Cried Wolf*. You don't want your kids to be whistle-blowers unless lost or in trouble.

CAN YOU KEEP A SECRET?

I visited a school where a policeman talked to some six-year-olds about men who might offer them sweets. The policeman made them promise never to keep a secret. That afternoon, the same class made tissue-paper flowers for Mother's Day. Their teacher told them it was important to keep them secret until Mother's Day, or Mom wouldn't be surprised. Pre-teens get muddled. You've probably noticed that little ones in particular can be very literal and so struggle to tell the difference between secrets with a sinister motive and good surprises. Next time you have a family meeting (Idea 29) establish a rule like "some things we never keep secret like hugs, kisses, or who ate the last chocolate cookie."

THE MYTH OF STRANGER DANGER

Teaching children about so-called stranger danger is a waste of time. The vast majority of abused children suffer at the hands of someone they know. Again, children's literal take on the world means their understanding of a stranger differs from yours. Who is a stranger? That helpful shopkeeper? The friendly classroom assistant? Auntie Joan's new boyfriend? Ingenious parents teach children to say no to anyone, stranger or not, who says or does anything that makes them frightened, confused, or uneasy.

"Be prepared. The meaning of that motto is that a scout must prepare himself by previous thinking out and practicing how to act on any accident or emergency so that he is never taken by surprise."
ROBERT BADEN-POWELL, founder of the Scouts, who was concerned with developing children's imaginations and allowing them to have adventures

Defining idea...

"How true Daddy's words were when he said, 'All children must look after their own upbringing.' Parents can only give good advice or put them on the right paths."
ANNE FRANK, *The Diary of a Young Girl*

Defining idea...

How did it go?

Q **When I was a kid I used to spend lots of time playing outside. But there are so many perverts now and I'm really afraid for my children. Am I wrong to keep them in?**

A *Stories about child abduction, rape, and murder are media obsessions so it's understandable that you worry. But it is important you remember that these tragic events are rare and very unlikely to happen to your pre-teens. Keeping kids indoors exposes them to other, less newsworthy risks. They become bored, miss out on friendships, develop fewer interests, and struggle socially in their teens and adulthood.*

Q **If I teach my son to say no to being touched, won't it make him less affectionate?**

A *It's a dilemma. Children are cuddly by nature. Hugs and snuggles ought to be a big part of every child's life, and sadly a minority of adults exploit that. It would be a disaster if he said no to all physical contact. Teach him to say no to touches he doesn't like, and never to keep them secret. If these conversations feel difficult, have a look at Idea 38,* Cigarettes, drugs, alcohol. *If he learns to look after himself, he'll be more comfortable socially, rather than less affectionate.*

40

Wicked stepparents

Wicked: spiteful, ill-tempered, malicious.
Wicked: excellent, remarkable, outstanding.
We'll help you step in the right direction.

Cinderella, Snow White, and Harry Potter are all persecuted by evil stepmothers. In books, ballets, films, and folklore, stepfamily life gets terrible press and is often misrepresented as second best.

But it's not all divided loyalties and power struggles. Pre-teens raised in stepfamilies have access to a larger extended family and maybe even another language or culture. An only child may have brothers and sisters for the first time.

THREE SECRETS OF WICKED STEPPARENTS

1. You can't hurry love
Don't expect stepchildren to cherish you immediately. In our experience, preschoolers will form an attachment to stepparents within a couple of years. As a rule of thumb, older pre-teens take up to as many years as they are old when the

Here's an idea for you... **Treat stepkids like royalty. The Queen of England has two birthdays, her actual one and an official one. If it's good enough for her it's good enough for your stepchildren.**

stepparent enters their life. So if your eleven-year-old stepdaughter hates you, there's no need to worry until after her twenty-first birthday. Pre-teens often feel they are being disloyal to their birth parents if they enjoy a stepparent's company. It helps if they never hear you criticize or put their biological parent down. The best stepparents in the world will never replace a birth parent who has died. If you're in this position, try thinking of yourself as an "extra" parent, rather than a replacement.

2. Create shared history and be creative with new traditions

Most nuclear families have photo albums. Looking back at these gives pre-teens a sense of stability and helps them remember special days. There's no reason why stepfamilies can't make special albums, too. We suggest everyone contributes a few photographs from their original family before adding ones of your newly blended family. Take disposable cameras on family days out. Stepbrothers and stepsisters may spend holidays with biological parents. Try to plan at least one holiday each year when the whole stepfamily is together.

Successful stepfamilies develop rituals that help ease the transition when children move between one parent's house to the other, and work to develop new and flexible ways to celebrate birthdays and holidays so children aren't caught in the middle.

3. Don't be too strict too early

When it comes to discipline, step carefully. It's confusing for children and stepparents when new stepparents do a lot of disciplining, rewrite the family rule book, and apply sanctions. Bringing up another person's pre-teen is hard, so don't worry if it takes twice as long as you expected before you can take on a disciplinary role.

JUST VISITING

Step-pre-teen interlopers, who spend weekends with their "real" dad, usually won't want his girlfriend tagging along. If you're a weekend stepmom, don't force yourself on the pre-teens. After three years of silent Sunday roasts, Judith bonded with her step-pre-teen visitors. "Gideon brought his bike with him and was very impressed that I could fix a puncture," she recalls, "and Abi and I went to the hairdresser for a girly Saturday morning." Check with the ex before transforming Rapunzel into a skinhead. A clear polish manicure at the local salon might be safer.

SUCCESS WITH THE EX

Drop the raised eyebrows. Making friends with your partner's ex can be the sassiest move a stepmom makes. It is easier for kids to get along with a stepmom if their mother is on speaking terms with you. If their mom doesn't trust you, why should they? One way to start is to ask her if the kids would like to invite friends for a sleepover when they next visit. Charlotte made friends with her husband's ex-wife, Amina: "She'd seen me as a younger, prettier rival with more cleavage, but once she found out I'm a lousy cook and can't play tennis, which her kids adore, she became a lot less rivalrous." Charlotte started by picking the pre-

One of the most common problems in stepfamily life stems from different parenting styles. It can be tough figuring out what works best, particularly if you don't agree. Check out IDEA 19, _Singing from the same song sheet_.

Try another idea...

"Two delinquent sons used to come round every weekend and wreck the place. I had to be nice to them of course. Wicked stepmother and all that."
DEBORAH MOGGACH, _The Ex Wives_

Defining idea...

187

Defining idea...

"Some stepmothers are shocked to discover that they feel resentment, anxiety, jealousy, indifference, or even downright dislike for their stepchildren. These negative feelings are perfectly normal, but they are difficult to admit and still more difficult to face."

PEARL KETOVER PRILIK,
Stepmothering, *Another Kind of Love*

Defining idea...

"Parents, especially stepparents, are sometimes a bit of a disappointment to their children. They don't fulfill the promise of their early years."

ANTHONY POWELL, novelist

teens up from Amina's house on Friday evenings on her way home from work: "I knew as a single mom she'd earn less and appreciate not having to fork out the train fare. Our doorstep handover evolved into coffee and a chat. It also meant I got to know the kids during the drive."

NEW ARRIVAL

A new baby binds a blended family together. Nice in theory. Myth in practice. If you decide to have a "yours" baby, tell the children first, preferably when they are together to minimize sibling splits and spats. It helps if they know about practicalities: moving, less money, sharing bedrooms. They won't like it, but they have more time to adjust so won't take it (all) out on the baby when she arrives.

Q **When I tell my stepson off, he ignores me or says "Mommy lets me do that." When I take away privileges, he does spiteful things, like putting honey on my underwear.**

How did it go?

A *Parental authority is related to the depth of the parent–child relationship. Your stepmom–stepson bond is weak, as you have such a brief shared history. A common mistake stepparents make is that they try to discipline stepchildren too early. Spend time building a relationship and leave the discipline to dad.*

Q **My boyfriend hardly sees his kids and when he does see them, they don't seem to know what to do together. How can I help him?**

A *It's sad that two years after divorce, one in two men have no contact with the family they left behind. If he doesn't know how to relate to his kids, help him out by reading Idea 42, Part-time parents, and Idea 52, Something for the weekend. On a practical note, it helps if he can stay friends with his ex and if you live within easy traveling distance.*

189

41

Smooth moves

Moving is stressful. There's so much for parents to do and think about. It's easy to see how pre-teens get (emotionally) left behind. Here's how to transform a potentially bumpy ride into an unforgettable adventure.

Maybe you think moving is exciting rather than upsetting and you're wondering what the fuss is about.

But once you've heard your pre-teens protest "I hate my new room" you'll know where we're coming from. While you're concentrating on practical problems, pre-teens are preoccupied with all the losses inherent in a move: friends, school, a favorite teacher, their bedrooms, and secret hideaways. Involving and preparing kids for a move isn't always easy. Granted, we're not suggesting pre-teens should pick your new place out of a real estate agent's window, but ever wondered how you can ease the transition? Wonder no more.

AS SOON AS YOU KNOW YOU ARE MOVING

See if you can broach the idea of moving by sneaking it into play. So if your daughters are busy with their dolls' house, talk to them about moving and what the dolls would need to do. We've found that parents who put off telling their children about an imminent move encounter more resistance later.

Here's an idea for you...

When it comes to bedrooms, pre-teen tastes are more sophisticated than ever. Ask for their help in planning their new bedrooms, choosing color schemes and decorating themes, and where to put furniture. A Disney duvet cover or Harry Potter pajama bag may make all the difference.

MONTHS BEFORE MOVING

Tell children about their new home. Even though pre-teens can't decide which home to buy or which area to move to, they can get involved in other ways, like choosing color schemes for their bedrooms. Older children might like a floor plan or to use an old shoebox to plan bedrooms to perfection. For children too little to take part in these sorts of decisions, try to keep the new room as similar to their old bedrooms as possible.

WEEKS BEFORE MOVING

Pre-teens appreciate magical outings to their new home and its surroundings. Try a treasure hunt with a twist. Prepare a list of local "treasures," like a petting zoo, their new school, an oak tree in the new neighborhood, and challenge your children to find them. Older children can look on a map to find parks and playgrounds. As well as showing them their new room, why not photograph it so they can show it off? During your book at bedtime, choose stories with moving plots. All these things normalize moving and help children look forward to it.

DAYS BEFORE MOVING

We know a little boy who saw his toys being packed up and worried they were being taken away. Younger children might need reminding that their toys are being boxed so they can be taken to their new home. Most pre-teens will be able to pack some non-fragile items themselves, like boxed games and soft toys. We'd advise against buying a new bed or other furniture before moving. Old familiar furniture, especially beds, instill deep feelings of warmth and security at a time that can be unsettling.

Moving house? Stressed out? If you are, chances are the rest of the family is, too. Check out IDEA 36, *Stress busters*.

Try another idea...

THE DAY YOU MOVE

If possible, see if your pre-teen can spend moving day with friends or family. You don't need us to tell you you're likely to be busy and not have time to play or explain. Children might want a special toy to keep them company. Pack a few party hats, firecrackers, and a string of lights into a plastic bag and keep it with you. When unpacking, we suggest you do the children's rooms first so they can retreat to them.

AFTER THE MOVE

Congratulations! You've arrived at your dream home. Create some good memories of the first night in your new camp. We're sure your cooking utensils will still be boxed up and know the last thing either of us would feel like doing is making a celebratory meal. So turn takeout into a celebration with your party hats, firecrackers, and lights.

"The ideal home: Big enough for you to hear the children, but not very well."
MIGNON MCLAUGHLIN, *The Second Neurotics Notebook*

Defining idea...

How did
it go?

Q **Our four-year-old daughter threw a big tantrum when we told her about moving to the city.**

A *It must be really tempting not to bring it up again, but try to gradually reintroduce the idea about living somewhere else. Find something really exciting in the new neighborhood, like a city farm or toy museum. Go for a picnic in a park in the new neighborhood, followed by a short walk, and "discover" this place, emphasizing the positives of living there. While it's good she has been able to let you know how she feels, tantrums are not an acceptable way of communicating, and you might like to have a look at Idea 11,* Tantrum taming.

Q **Is it better to move during school vacations or while classes are in session?**

A *The jury's still out on this one. Children who move at the end of the school year have the whole summer vacation to get used to the idea and have a new start with the rest of the class. The biggest downside of moving during school breaks is that children have to spend them in limbo, without their old friends and before they've had a chance to make new ones at school. If you can choose, we'd go for the vacations because it minimizes learning disruptions, but provides opportunities for them to socialize in the new neighborhood.*

42

Part-time parents

Fed up with feeling frozen out after business trips? Buying an overpriced model airplane or Bratz doll might make you feel less guilty, but it won't thaw those frosty pre-teen hearts. We've learned secrets from successful part-timers, and we're willing to pass them on.

Separation, divorce, being a member of the armed forces, working abroad, frequent business trips, and long-distance truck driving are just a few of the many reasons people find themselves being a part-time parent.

FAMILY REUNIONS

Coming home only to be given the cold shoulder by the pre-teens sucks. We've found knowing what to expect helps part-time parents with awkward reunions. Babies cry and sometimes pull back when a part-time parent returns and tries to cuddle them. Try not to take it personally. Even if you've only been away for a short time, it's normal for babies to be mistrustful and treat you like a stranger. If your baby appears not to recognize you, speak to her, giving her a chance to recognize your voice.

Here's an idea for you...

Rituals help pre-teens adjust to change. Why not develop a special routine for reunions? It might be going bowling the evening after the kids come to stay, or having a cake with candles when Mommy comes home.

Toddlers are different. They are more likely to demand lots of attention, pushing you to the limit with tantrums or making you feel guilty for being away. This isn't done to spite you, but because toddlers often experience separation anxiety, and may worry you'll go away again and abandon them. School-age children can snub part-time parents on your return. Used to having the "home" parent to themselves, they may find ways of getting extra attention, like tummy aches.

On the other hand, part-time parents are sometimes built up out of all proportion. The prodigal dad returning laden with exotic gifts from far-flung shores gets all the kids' admiration, while the parent left to do the day-to-day stuff lives in his shadow. When prodigal dad comes back for good, it can be hard to live up to his hero reputation.

HOME AND AWAY

We suggest that the "away" parent either emails regularly or phones at prearranged times. Pre-teens need to have written or telephone contact at least twice a week, ideally three times. There are lots of ways to share feelings, news, and experiences. Mel often works away with a touring opera company. At home, Mel's children have

Defining idea...

"If you have never been hated by your children, you have never been a parent."
BETTE DAVIS

a big photo of him over a whiteboard. Whenever they think of something they would like to tell him, their mom writes it on the whiteboard, and next time they speak to him, it acts as a reminder of all their news. Kelly and Louis photocopy school reports, ballet certificates, and star-charts and send them to Dad so he stays in touch with what they are doing while he's away. When Michael's mom was abroad for a conference, he was upset that she wouldn't see his archery trophy as it was only given for one week at a time. His dad helped him take a digital photograph of it and they emailed it to Mom. Dianne's parents are divorced. Her first tooth came out when she was staying with her dad over the holidays, so they sent it to Mom in a matchbox, so she wouldn't miss out. Sean started to learn to play the piano while his dad was posted away with the army, so he surprised him with a homemade tape. Tapes can work in both directions. Enid is a judge. For several weeks each year, she has to travel around the country, hearing cases on the northern circuit. She sends home a weekly audio diary of her week. Zoe's dad is a tour leader. Before he goes away, he leaves her a laminated map. Every few days, she receives a postcard, telling her where he is, and

Trouble with toddler tantrums every time you come home? Stop them in their tracks with IDEA 11, *Tantrum taming.*

Try another idea...

"Benjamin never holds my absences against me. Too little still. He always greets me with helpless delight like a fan windmilling his arms at a Hollywood premiere. Not his sister though. Emily is five years old and full of jealous wisdom. Mommy's return is always the cue for an intricate sequence of snubs and punishments. 'Actually, Paula reads me that story.' 'But I want daddy to give me a bath.' Wallis Simpson got a warmer welcome from the Queen Mother than I get from Emily after a business trip."
ALLISON PEARSON, journalist

Defining idea...

197

she sticks a pin into that part of the map, tracing his journey until he comes home. He also buys her a special calendar, where she checks off the remaining days.

CAN WE STAY UP LATE TONIGHT?

It's easy to let discipline slip when you're doing it alone, but families who discipline differently when one parent is away have more problems getting their kids to behave. Kids are more likely to test boundaries when circumstances change, partly because they feel afraid and out of control. They need you to enforce rules now more than usual.

How did it go?

Q **I work night shifts, so my partner has been putting the kids to bed and getting them up in the morning. Now that I'm working days, I feel like spending a bit more time with them in the evenings and letting them stay up longer. My partner wants them to stick to their usual bedtime. What do you think?**

A *It's important you don't inadvertently undermine your partner, who has been doing so much parenting while you were working nights. If you're having trouble presenting a united front, have a look at Idea 19, Singing from the same song sheet.*

43

Little chef

Kids helping in the kitchen don't have to be a recipe for disaster. The sooner you can get them hanging around the kitchen sink, the better. Who knows, they may even do the dishes.

Cooking makes children more independent. It also improves self-esteem, and makes them more dexterous and attentive to details. Buying ingredients teaches budgeting. Weighing and measuring ingredients helps with math.

Pre-teens who follow a recipe carefully have delicious treats to reward their efforts. Planning, hygiene, nutrition, presentation skills, and learning to do the dishes are other things they might pick up, but don't count on it. And if it goes wrong, dads or dogs will usually eat the evidence.

KITCHEN HANDS

If you sit your toddler on the work surface when you cook and let her join in, she'll get the idea that cooking is fun. Small children love mixing and stirring. It'll be

Here's an idea for you...

Once your pre-teen can shape Play-Doh, she can make the petit fours for your next dinner party. Color marzipan with a few drops of food coloring. Kids like to do the next part: Knead the color into the marzipan until it is evenly colored. With orange, yellow, green, and red marzipan, they'll be able to make a selection of fruit and veggies, molding little spheres of marzipan as if it was any other modeling material. Use cloves to make stalks on apples and pears and push them all the way in to make the bottom of an orange. They look stunning in petit four cases. If you don't have a party planned, they can be made in advance and stored in a box with layers of tissue paper between them. Your pre-teen might also like to make animals to decorate an iced cake for a special occasion.

messy, but she'll love you for it. Rosie tells her toddler triplets that if they're good while she cooks, they can add parsley garnish. Older pre-teens can move on to grating, then chopping.

We're not saying that letting your toddler mash the potatoes is going to turn him into a three-star chef, but he'll have a massive head start when he flies the nest, feeding hungry students or impressing girlfriends and their parents.

MORE THAN A MERE TRIFLE

Everyone remembers Rice Krispie treats. But pre-teen baking doesn't have to start and end with mixing marshmallows and cereal. Pancakes, pecan brownies, fudge, and truffles are simple enough for a six-year-old to make with supervision. Your pre-teen can impress relatives with homemade chocolates. Help her melt a bar of chocolate and pour into clean small molds usually used for making plaster of Paris models.

Rocket Popsicles are easy, too. You don't need special molds. Pre-teens can fill empty yogurt containers with diluted fruit juice and insert a chopstick for a Popsicle stick. Your kids will need to dilute fruit juice in different colors. Apple, cranberry, and orange look striking. Pour one color juice two fingers depth into each container and freeze. Once it's frozen solid, add another layer in a different color. When they're two fingers' depth from the top, finish with a layer of melted chocolate to catch any drips in case the pops melt faster than your kids and their friends can eat them.

NAMING DISHES

Bill Bursell's dad helped him layer homemade banana ice cream into tall glasses, squirted a bit of cream and chocolate sauce on top, and they called it William's Wednesday Sundae. Jennifer put gummy bears in Jell-O and named it Jenny's Jiggly Jelly. Giving recipes names encourages little cooks and develops their creativity.

...and another....

Next time you have a scrap of pastry left over after making a flan, pie, buns, or anything else, get the kids to make biscuits or cookies with it. Rolling out pastry and cutting out shapes with cookie cutters is great, but if you don't have any, they can use a jam jar or even an egg cup to cut out circles. Brushing savory biscuits with egg or milk and sprinkling with poppy seeds and the thinnest sliver of cheese gives them real bite. Sweet pastries cut into heart shapes, baked, and half dipped into melted plain chocolate make good presents when wrapped in a twist of cellophane. While the cookies bake, pre-teens can add a zing by using the heart cutter as a stencil to make a matching cardboard gift tag.

201

Try another idea...

Planning a party? Pre-teens can help. Go to IDEA 47, *Perfect picnics, parties, and packed lunches.*

Defining idea...

"Let's face it, if they're normal kids, they'll be scoffing chocolate and chips and spurious concoctions of sugared drinks throughout the day. So let's get them cooking their own treats and learning what goes into them. And if they make a dreadful mess, who cares? That's what soap and water are for. Let them bake cake!"
MARY CONTINI, director of Italian delicatessen Valvona and Crolla

CHEAT'S EATS

Our favorite kitchen appliances—breadmaker and ice-cream maker—are literally child's play to use. It's a breeze for pre-teens to whizz up chocolate concoctions or warm, spicy raisin bread. Once they've got the hang of it, experimenting with unusual ingredients or combinations is sweetly simple.

PIZZA FEATURES

From around eight years upward, pre-teens can make their own pizza dough in your breadmaker. Younger kids can roll out dough or at least flour the rolling surface. Top with a mixture of heated chopped tomatoes, basil, and fried onions. Then children can make faces out of toppings. Circles of tomato or pepperoni eyes, anchovy eyebrows, mushroom noses, and red pepper mouths are just a few serving suggestions. We all have days when we can't be bothered to make dough, so it's worth keeping a few plain pizza bases at the bottom of the freezer.

Q   **My ancestors are Chinese and I'd like the kids to learn some traditional dishes, but so far they're not interested. What can I try?**

How did it go?

A   *Food is a brilliant way into another culture. Try holding a themed evening. Make everyone dress up in silk dressing gowns and paper hats, eat with chopsticks, and serve traditional dim sum. Show the kids how to make jasmine tea. Spend the afternoon making other things for the party with them, like Chinese paper lanterns or cutting out a big red dragon to hang on the wall, and sneak off into the kitchen for "important cooking." They'll follow. If they get into this, have an all-day breakfast party on a Sunday afternoon, where everyone hangs out in their pajamas all day, reads papers or comics, and cooks together.*

44

Smart shopping

Murder in the malls or smiles in the aisles? Shopping can be either. Teaching pre-teens to become savvy shoppers is one of the underrated pleasures of parenting.

Shopping should be fun. However, if you wander around your local supermarket, you'll notice some families find it anything but. The key is whether children are treated as nuisances who get in the way or as little helpers.

HAPPY SHOPPERS

Next time you make your family shopping list, involve your kids. Questions like, "What do we need?" should get ideas coming. If they only think of sweets, don't give up, but try, "Great, desserts are done, but what about main meals?" Tell children if they are good in the supermarket, they can have a treat afterward. You might try having a separate heading of "treats" on your list. Let them all choose something small, like a bag of chips or bubble gum, and make sure they see you've written it down. When you get to the supermarket, a little one can be in charge of holding the list and checking off items with a special felt pen or crayon, while older

Here's an idea for you... **If visits to large supermarkets are stressing you and the kids out, why not make shorter and more frequent visits to local shops? Specialist butchers, bakers, organic grocers, and candy stores are being steamrollered by the big boys and it might be the only chance your kids have to see small community stores in action. Older children can go on errands to learn independence. Give your son a list of a few items you need and give him enough money to cover it. He'll learn to find items, line up at the register, pay, count change, and check it against the receipt.**

siblings go on missions to find the next item. Another child can keep a running total on a pocket calculator. Once all the items are checked, let them find their treats, if they've behaved. It's important not to give in and let naughty children have their treat, or they won't see the point in being good next time. If your children are still too small for this activity, sit them in the cart, but give a running commentary of what you are buying. Talk about the ingredients and what you will be looking for next, to develop language and nutrition knowledge. Ask them to pick some items like cans of soup and put them in the cart. Noisy food, like a bag of dried pasta or box of cereal, can be surprisingly entertaining for babies to sit and rattle. Try taking a picture book for warding off toddler trouble.

WINDOW-SHOPPING

A mom we admire taught her children they couldn't have everything they want. She takes them window-shopping. They know beforehand that they're "only looking." If they forget and ask for something, she reminds them: "Today we're window-shopping, but another time we might buy something." Her children are less greedy and impulsive when they do go shopping with purchases in mind.

HEY, BIG SPENDERS

Want to buy your pre-teens some fashionable clothes but stuck for cash? Cheap frills can be had at online auctions, secondhand shops, and yard sales. You're also more likely to find one-off outfits and vintage party dresses. Ooh la la.

OUT OF POCKET

For pre-teens, pocket money can be a problem as well as a solution. Before letting them spend real pocket money, practice by playing shop. Sadly, lessons like checking change before it's too late, finding the best value, avoiding expensive mistakes, and being patient enough to save up for what they really want, rather than blowing their cash on candy at payday, are best learned by experience. So stop talking and let them shop till the penny drops.

We've found children are usually motivated to shop for ingredients if they choose the recipe. See IDEA 43, *Little chef.*

Try another idea...

Toddler tantrums in aisle seven? Checkout IDEA 11, *Tantrum taming.*

...and another...

"Never get so fascinated by the extraordinary that you forget the ordinary."
MAGDALEN NABB, crime writer and children's author

Defining idea...

"Years ago a person, he was unhappy, didn't know what to do with himself—he'd go to church, start a revolution, something. Today, you're unhappy? Can't figure it out? What's the salvation? Go shopping."
ARTHUR MILLER, *The Price*

Defining idea...

207

FAMILY FURNISHINGS

Taking children furniture shopping increases their sense of ownership in your home, making them more likely to help you redecorate and less likely to jump on the sofa.

We think the earlier you involve pre-teens in choosing furniture and accessories, the better. Often, they have excellent taste and judgment and can make your home less jaded and more razzle-dazzle.

How did it go?

Q **We take our two children shopping with us. Unfortunately, they get competitive and squabble and it gets really embarrassing. What do you suggest?**

A *Why not divide the shopping list in two? Split the family into two teams, with one child going with each parent, and meet at the register with your respective carts.*

Q **I'd like to let my daughter shop on her own, but it isn't safe in our neighborhood.**

A *She can still learn important skills if you go shopping together, but encourage her to choose something for herself and pay with her pocket money.*

45

Music matters

Shakespeare called it the "food of love." There's more to music than great tunes and throbbing rhythms. Music is one meal that needs to be on every pre-teen's menu.

Music helps children make sense of the world. Singing simple songs teaches children about grammar, syntax, and subtle nuances of tone. Makes those endless repetitions of "Row, row, row your boat" seem a bit like rocket science.

We sing to babies, but tend to stop as children get older. But keep those tunes coming. Your musical children will make friends more easily, as they'll have superior social skills, higher self-esteem, and greater self-confidence.

MOSTLY MOZART

Classical music, and Mozart's music in particular, has been credited with improving pre-teen's lives, stimulating mental growth, reducing stress, helping them sleep, boosting memory, and developing creativity. Bring on the baroque.

Here's an idea for you...

Why not suggest your musical progeny organize and present a musical evening? An audience of grandparents and tone-deaf neighbors and pets will provide the necessary affirmation. A rendition of the opening bars of Wagner's *Ring* on homemade instruments is bound to bring tears to any music lover's eyes, and complement the concert afterward. Nights like these will never be forgotten, we promise.

Defining idea...

"Children who take part in music develop higher levels of social cohesion and understanding of themselves and others, and the emotional aspect of musical activities seems to be beneficial for developing social skills like empathy."
DR. ALEXANDRA LAMONT, lecturer in the psychology of music

MAKING MUSIC

Encourage pre-school children by playing songs and letting them accompany the tape with homemade instruments.

Drum
You'll need:
- A cereal box
- String
- Two wooden spoons

Make a hole in either end of the box. Thread the string through and adjust it so the drum hangs around your child's neck at waist height. Give him the drumstick spoons and get marching.

Kitchen cymbals
You'll need:
- Two pot or pan lids

Bang together.

Macaroni maracas
You'll need:
- A handful of dried macaroni
- Two small (empty) ice cream containers with lids. Put a little pasta in each container. Shake, rattle, and roll.

Jam jar jammin'

You'll need:

- A wooden spoon
- Twelve empty jam jars (pasta sauce jars will do)

Fill each jar with a finger's depth more water than the previous one. The lower the water level, the lower the pitch when struck with a spoon.

No ordinary oboe

You'll need:

- Long cardboard tube that you get inside rolls of wrapping paper, aluminum foil, or plastic wrap
- Wax paper or tracing paper
- Elastic band
- Knitting needle

Cover one end of the tube with wax paper and fix in place with the elastic band. Poke a row of holes down one side of the tube with a knitting needle, and hum into the open end. When you've composed yourself, let the kids give it a try.

If one of your children is nervous about performing, why not refer to IDEA 36, *Stress busters*.

Try another idea...

"If we do not provide adequate opportunities for our children to learn and participate in music, we are depriving them of something priceless. It is important that such provision should be made as early as possible. I am entirely in favor of recent methods of teaching children to play string instruments from an early age. Not all of them will turn into competent violinists, viola players, cellists, or double bass players; but those who do will taste the delight of playing chamber music, that which there is no greater pleasure."

DR. ANTHONY STORR, *Music and the Mind*

Defining idea...

211

Shoebox strummin'

You'll need:

- A shoebox (discard the lid)
- Six wide elastic bands
- A wooden spoon

Stretch the elastic bands around the shoebox and strum with the wooden spoon.

INSTRUMENTAL BENEFITS

We've heard neuroscientists suggest playing the piano enhances pre-teens' spatial–temporal reasoning. To you and us, this means they're better able to visualize and transform objects in space and time. Sounds offbeat? Music involves ratio, proportions, and fractions, so why shouldn't these skills transfer?

Six to eight years is the optimum age for your child to learn her first instrument, or join his first choir. At this age, pre-teens have a better memory for music and are able to learn sight-reading. Children who practice an instrument daily develop concentration that helps with their schoolwork. Mastering a musical instrument improves hand–eye coordination and also builds a sense of accomplishment, which raises a pre-teen's self-worth.

Q **Ben, eight, nagged us for ages to get a piano and piano lessons. We told him that if we did he would have to practice. He stuck it out for about two weeks and then refused to go near the piano room. He seems to like his teacher, but he'll never get the hang of the instrument unless he practices.**

How did it go?

A *A common tale and we're afraid there's not much you can do. Some children take to an instrument like a duck to water while others, like Ben, struggle or give up without much of a fight. Push him too hard and you could put him off music forever. Why not suggest he joins a church or school choir where music is easier for individuals?*

Q **We have two girls, Nicola (age eleven) and Gemma (age nine). Both are good musicians but Gemma is clearly more gifted than her older sister, who dutifully labors away. It's starting to cause some resentment as teachers and other parents make a big fuss over our younger daughter. How can we ensure that Nicola doesn't feel completely overshadowed?**

A *The brutal truth is that you can't. Life is unfair, especially when talent is being handed out. It might help if they played different but musically compatible instruments, like piano and violin or harpsichord and flute. As a parent your job is to value both children and minimize unnecessary competition.*

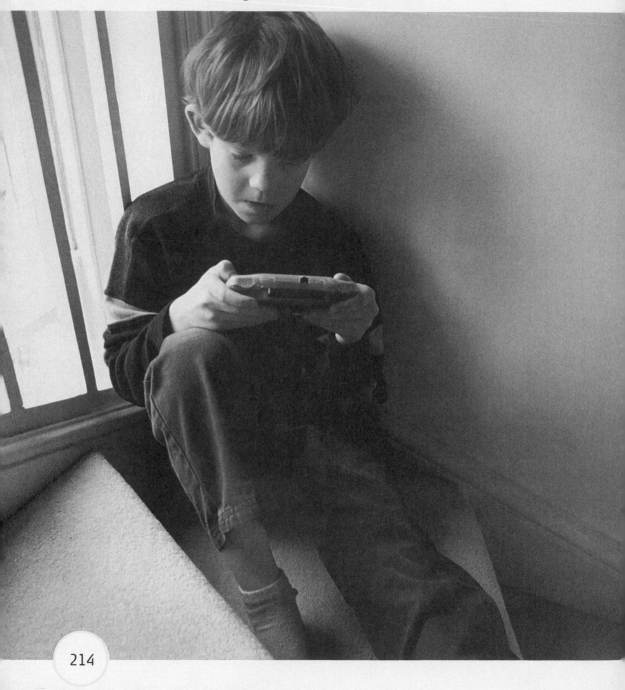

46

Save it for a rainy day

It's raining, it's pouring, and your kids complain that it's boring. Not with these tricks up your sleeve.

Once your pre-teens have built a camp under the dining-room table, they'll feel that's what rainy days were made for. They'll need to gather up all your big blankets, bedspreads, quilts, pillows, and cushions. Camps are great for doing secret pre-teen stuff in. We won't tell you what that is, but if you knock and ask nicely, they might just let a grown-up in.

Younger pre-teens love blowing big bubbles. It's simple to set up. Pour a little dishwashing liquid into a bowl and show your children how to froth it up with a balloon whisk or egg beater. While they whisk away, bend a wire coat hanger into a giant bubble wand. Just pull out the oval-shaped part into something resembling a circle, and straighten out the hanger to make a small handle. Slotted spoons are

Here's an idea for you...

While the weather's horrible, why not catch up with some housework? Pre-teens will help, especially if you involve young kids in a new game: sorting laundry. Toddlers are able to sort all the socks into one pile, while older children can do something more ambitious, like folding. This teaches pre-teens how to put things into categories, which is the basis of science. We wouldn't leave pre-teens to sort dirty clothes into colored and white washes.

useful, too, for blowing itsy-bitsy bubbles. Can anyone catch a bubble without it bursting? If, after an hour or so your kids get bored, teach them how to play "washing kitchen surfaces." Toddlers in particular think this is a good game. Show them how to wipe surfaces with a sponge and wring it out. And should they tire of that, there's always the bathroom sink.

It's easy to change the color of another gray day. Pick a different color and make that your theme for the day. Our friends the Murrays decided to have a brown day with their pre-teens. They all ate sausages for breakfast, painted their nails with brown nail polish (yes, even the boys), used brown crayons to make rubbings, made peanut butter sandwiches and chocolate milk for lunch, counted brown cars passing by the window, and made beautiful brown collages by cutting pictures of pinecones and autumn leaves out of dad's old *National Geographic* magazines.

For older pre-teens, try to keep one or two projects going that can be whipped out of the closet and worked on whenever the weather turns bad. Linette's mom lets her use her sewing box on rainy days. She loves making doll clothes out of remnants and her dad's old silk handkerchiefs. George is good at potato printing, so his dad always keeps a batch of blank cards in the house. When it's wet outside,

George often prints a batch of cards, which his parents use as thank-you notes during the year. Wendy and Polly spent a wet August vacation making Christmas presents for their grandparents.

It's summer vacation. The weather's foul. Your kids are whining. You wish you were away on vacation. Time for an indoor beach party. Everyone wears sunglasses and sun hats. Put on swimsuits, spread beach towels out on the living room, and eat an indoor picnic lunch. Paddle in the bath, but watch out for jellyfish. Rub on after-sun lotion; the smell always cheers people up. If your kids really get into it, they might want to make some postcards. Ice cream and lemonade round off a day at the beach perfectly.

Hold a photo shoot. Digital cameras allow even you to turn the simplest point-and-click pics into masterpieces, so don't worry about camera shake, red eye, or thumbs in the frame. It needs some setting up, but if you keep all the stuff together in one place, you can set up your studio while the kids raid their dressing-up box. You need a black or white backdrop like a bedsheet or quilt. Tape it to the ceiling with masking tape, or hang it from a bookcase so a big area is covered. It helps if you have a couple of studio lamps that you can pick up fairly cheaply in secondhand stores. There are lots of ways to position the lamps, but we suggest you

Defining idea...

"Play is often talked about as if it were a relief from serious learning. But for children, play is serious learning. Play is really the work of childhood."
FRED ROGERS, host of *Mister Rogers' Neighborhood*

Try another idea...

You'll find some more suggestions about how to keep your kids occupied, happy, and stimulated in IDEA 52, *Something for the weekend.*

experiment, lighting your pre-teens from different angles while they strike different poses and dress up. If you have trouble with the photo software, under-tens will usually figure it out.

When the rain has stopped, send pre-teens outside wearing rain boots to splash in all the puddles or hunt for snails and watch the trails they make.

Q **We had a great day but the kids were so overexcited they couldn't settle down.**

A *Oops. Try a quieting down game (see Idea 15, Generation games) or doing fewer activities next time.*

47

Perfect picnics, parties, and packed lunches

Same old sandwiches and spaghetti? Solve these culinary crises and turn humdrum meals into magnificent feasts.

Planning a party menu or picnic can feel overwhelming. It did for us, too, until the truth hit us: Picnic baskets are just like massive lunch boxes and parties are indoor picnics. If you can fill a lunch box, you can feed a tent full of pre-teens.

PERFECT PICK-ME-UPS

Food that pre-teens can pick up and eat with their hands is perfect picnic, party, and lunch box food: fruit salad, pancakes, strips of green pepper, small cakes, cucumber sticks, four squares of chocolate, mini pepperoni, cookies, cupcakes, or wontons. When it comes to pre-teen's food, think small and they'll think you're the greatest. Remember the cocktail parties you went to before you had kids? The sort

Here's an idea for you... **Cook a little extra when you make dinner and there'll be enough for lunch. For example, if you make quiche, let the kids make little ones in small flan tins. Or, if you have a barbecue, throw on a couple of extra drumsticks. We have it on excellent pre-teen authority that they taste even better cold. Split and fill pita bread with leftover salad, pop in a few cherry tomatoes, and they'll have the best meal in class.**

of hors d'oeuvres and nibbles served are ideal for pre-teens. Falafel, salmon blinis, and prawn vol-au-vents may be acquired tastes, so start sneaking them into lunch boxes early. The other secret is variety. Put grapes in your kid's lunch box every day, and they'll turn into raisins. Instead, try pear today, plum tomorrow.

SANDWICH SHOW-OFFS

Make movie-star sandwiches by cutting ordinary sandwiches into star shapes with a cookie cutter. If you can't get pre-teens to eat brown bread, don't use your loaf, use their's. We've found pre-teens are more likely to eat exotic breads like rye, date, and walnut or oatmeal loaf if they've baked it themselves in a breadmaker. We don't care what your domestic science teacher said, sandwiches don't need to be bread, filling, bread. Triple-decker combos using three kinds of bread are at least three times tastier.

FABULOUS FILLINGS

The best fillings are ones pre-teens can help make. We love:

- **Egg and homegrown cress.** Seed to sandwich in just three weeks (see Idea 32, *How does your garden grow?*).
- **Bacon, lettuce, and tomato.** Pre-teens can grill bacon, chop tomatoes, and even grow their own lettuce.

- **Avocado and chicken.** On Sunday evenings, get the kids to mash a couple of avocados while you chop roast dinner leftovers. Avocado contains natural antidepressants so it's perfect for banishing Monday blues.

Pre-teens who prepare their own lunches are less likely to complain about them and more likely to learn lots of other life skills. See IDEA 43, *Little chef*.

Try another idea...

CUT THEM LOOSE IN THE KITCHEN

Shake it baby
Pre-teens can whip up amazing drinks in blenders. Strawberry yogurt smoothies, coconut milkshakes, and fruit cocktails are fun and easy to make, but also much healthier than sodas and sports drinks.

Salad days
Kids can easily make salad by pouring vegetable stock over couscous or bulgar wheat and then fluffing it up with a fork. They can add chopped vegetables, cold meat, or anything else that tickles their taste buds. Mix in some natural yogurt, a squirt of lemon juice, and maybe a sprig or two of mint. Alternatively, use small pasta shells as a salad base. Pasta salad is ideal for using up leftover pizza toppings.

An apple a day...
Is very tedious. Why not let your pre-teen make his own fruit salads? Encourage him to experiment with tastes and textures. Pre-teens we know have come up with mango and cranberry; kiwi, melon, papaya, and orange

"There are times when parenthood seems to be nothing more than feeding the hand that bites you."
PETER DE VRIES, *The Tunnel of Love*

Defining idea...

221

marmalade; pink grapefruit, blood orange, and raspberry; and, the one we liked best, peaches, strawberries, and blueberries.

It's a wrap
Tortilla wraps, tacos, and pitas are perfect for parceling out leftovers into a second meal. Even a simple meal like grilled fish and roasted peppers tastes terrific in a tortilla with a splash of salsa or cool cucumber and yogurt.

Cupcakes
Pre-teens can pour cupcake mix into petit four cases: half the size, half the fat, but twice as nice. Worried about their sugar intake and unable to get them to eat anything healthy? Try putting carrot cake or banana bread mixture into cupcake tins. Dust with powdered sugar and your secret's safe.

Twisted thinking
Who said cheese straws have to be straight? Pre-teens can shape them into their initials and sprinkle with sesame seeds. Having a party? Get your kids to write down the initials of all the guests and get twisting.

How did
it go?

Q I send my daughter to school with crisp lettuce leaves and freshly baked bread, but she says it all goes soggy by lunchtime. Short of nagging the school to get a fridge, what can I do?

A *Doesn't sound very appetizing, but it's what happens in kid's lunch boxes when stored at classroom temperature. Freezing small cartons of juice before putting one in the lunch box in the morning helps keep lunches cool and food fresh.*

48

Arty facts

We're not promising that every pre-teen who picks up a paintbrush will become the next Picasso, but anyone who plays with colors, charcoal, chalk, crayons, or collage develops new ways of communicating and imagining.

Pre-teens who start drawing when they are young have more opportunity to practice hand movements needed for writing. Forget those thousand different shades of green crayon selections. Six short, fat crayons and some paper are all you need to get toddlers started.

CANVASS A TODDLER

When you introduce paints for the first time, start with one color initially, then two. Hand- and footprints are a messy and tactile introduction for toddlers not yet dextrous enough to use brushes. If you squirt a little dishwashing liquid into poster paints, they'll wash off your children, clothes, and furniture more easily. Toddlers paint in one of two styles: Mark Rothko or Jackson Pollock. Prepared canvas, already stretched and stapled to a board, is sold fairly inexpensively in art shops. What are you waiting for?

Here's an idea for you... **You don't need to buy lots of expensive sketching paper from specialist art shops just yet. Rolls of baking paper, the back of junk mail, or spare wallpaper is perfect.**

...and another... **Why not invest in a large frame that you can use to present special artwork? We suggest you change the display every month or so. Pre-teens can make more ornate frames by sticking dried pasta onto cardboard. If they paint them gold or silver, they look spectacular. Experiment with different types of pastas. We think minestrone shapes set off small portraits, whereas macaroni tubes seem to be better for landscapes. Coffee jar lids also make good frames. Pictures may need to be cut to fit, but the depth of these frames makes them perfect for displaying three-dimensional work.**

...and yet another... **Paint a wall with chalkboard paint and let everyone draw with chalk.**

Pre-teens can design their own blank postcards. Younger children can make very striking ones using one of these techniques:

- Finger painting: Dip fingers into thick poster paint and avoid furniture.
- Leaf prints: Dip leaves in paint and print onto paper.
- Straw-blowing: Chase a blob of really runny paint all over a big piece of paper.

Fruit-printed cards can be used for playing games afterward. You'll need around twenty blank cards and ten different types of fruit or vegetables for printing: onions, leeks, carrots, apples, pears, peppers, and oranges work well. Coat the fruit in thick paint and print. Once pre-teens have practiced on scrap paper, they'll know how hard to press and can print pairs of matching cards. It's best to use a different color for each vegetable. When the cards are dry, cover in clear plastic or take them to a stationery store to be laminated.

COMMISSION A PORTRAIT

Pre-teens are flattered when asked to paint the family or a new member such as a pet. Why not commission your child to paint a portrait from a photograph to surprise someone for a special occasion, like a golden wedding anniversary or thirtieth birthday?

It's really simple to make salt dough with pre-teens. Mix equal quantities of salt and flour, add a bit of olive oil and water, and knead. If it feels sticky, add a bit of flour. If it feels rough, add a drop of water or oil. Pre-teens can mold it like clay, making figures, animals, or three-dimensional pictures. Produced a salt dough masterpiece? Bend a paper clip into a hook and push into the back. Bake the dough in a low oven for about an hour. Once it's cool, kids can paint it with poster paints. Varnish, dry, and hang by the paper clip hook. No masterpiece today? Never mind, just squish it up and start again. Wrapped in plastic wrap, salt dough keeps in the fridge for about eight weeks, as the salt prevents it from getting moldy.

MULTISTORY MULTIMEDIA

Looking for an art project that can last all weekend or even all vacation? Multistory multimedia is not constrained by time or space. The idea is for pre-teens to make a miniature world, using all their art skills and developing new ones. This isn't just about little girls

Defining idea...

"Children between the ages of two and seven are very imaginative. This is the best period for the development of imagination, creativity, and thinking abilities."
CHIAM HENG KENG

Try another idea...

Why not play games with fruit-printed cards? IDEA 15, *Generation games,* **has instructions for Memory and Snap.**

Defining idea...

"Children have a natural antipathy to books. Handicraft should be the basis of education. Boys and girls should be taught to use their hands to make something and they would be less apt to destroy and be mischievous."
OSCAR WILDE

making a second-rate dollhouse. We know kids who have made an artist's studio, hat shop, patisserie, and secondhand car garage. Pre-teens need about a dozen shoeboxes. If you haven't got a friend like Imelda Marcos, ask at a local shoe store. Pile them high to make minimalist studios, or stick in a two-up, two-down formation, perhaps with a garage and conservatory. Once the basic structure's in place, they can get to work on the interior, recycling household castoffs. Raisin boxes, cereal boxes, sticky-backed plastic, pipe cleaners, and bottle lids can all be turned into almost anything.

For example, an empty margarine tub makes a bath, empty matchboxes stuck together make a chest of drawers, pictures cut out of magazines become artwork for the walls. Little mirrors can be made out of a piece of aluminum foil.

How did it go?

Q **Megan, who is five, used to scribble away happily. Recently, she's become very frustrated with her artwork, becoming annoyed when her pictures don't turn out as she planned and comparing her efforts unfavorably with other children.**

A *This is normal and not a sign of low self-esteem, as parents often fear. Younger children love making marks on paper and that is an end in itself. When pre-teens reach Megan's age, they realize that their pictures symbolize and stand for things. Admire her good efforts; praise her when it goes well. It also helps if she's left to paint for its own sake, rather than always asking her what her picture is of.*

49

Putting pen to paper

Writing works wonders. It's a tool for learning across artificial subject boundaries and far beyond the confines of classrooms. Let pre-teens write what they see and know and they'll easily debate, discuss, compare, and create. Power to the pencil.

Pre-teens who write have a creative way to explore their world, unravel ideas, cope with difficult feelings, and deliver messages to friends, teachers, and family. Pre-teens who write well have power and choices.

RESULT

The best way to encourage pre-teens to start writing can be summed up in a single word: results. Once your son realizes that a well-written thank-you letter to Auntie Fateha results in better birthday presents than ones his cousins get who don't bother to write, you're in business.

Pre-teens might not know what to say or how to lay out a letter. You may be tempted just to get them to copy one you've already written, but it's better in the long run to

Here's an idea for you...

If your children are feeling despondent with their early efforts, show them how much better it is than the stuff you were producing at their age. When Peter's mother was cleaning her house she discovered some of his old school exercise books. His English homework was awful. He showed one to his children, Mandy and Emma. They could see right away how much better their writing skills were.

ask open questions like: How did you feel when Grandpa bought you the Playstation? What did you like best about the books Uncle Jude sent? If they get stuck after writing "How are you?" suggest they describe the sort of day they are having, what other family members are doing, and what they're going to be up to over the weekend. Once they've captured their thoughts on the page, help with any spelling if they ask you. Grandparents treasure handwritten letters; some induce tears if carefully constructed. Idiosyncratic spelling and grammar are cherished.

...and another...

Pre-teen with writer's block? Coax the muse by playing Scrabble. After the game, leave the board out and have a short story competition. The rule? All the words on the board have to be in the story.

For that individual touch, your pre-teen could make personalized stationery on your home computer. Stickers on the backs of envelopes make good seals for pre-teens too young for a real wax sealing set. Thank-you letters don't have to be folded. Eleven-year-old Ben likes to roll his up like a scroll and send it in a cardboard tube, sold for sending posters.

Once your kids have perfected their letter-writing skills on friends and family, it's time to prove the power of the pencil. Help your pre-teen write a letter to her favorite author. Send it via the publisher. In our experience they are always forwarded and there's nothing like a reply from a real writer to encourage young talent. There may be other advantages: advance notice of the next title or an invitation to a signing or other special event. Maybe he'll even have a character named after him.

READ ALL ABOUT IT

Ten-year-old Gordon wrote to his local paper when a developer threatened to build offices on the site of a playground. Local schools acted and started a petition. The office development went up elsewhere.

DEAR DIARY

Pre-teens writing in a diary or journal can confess secret dreams, desires, and aspirations, or recount who said what on the playground and list what was served for supper. There are two problems with dairies: Parents snoop in them and pre-teens tire of them. Get rid of both problems with a family diary that everyone writes in after special occasions, like going abroad, sports events, or Hanukkah. Recording the whole family's recollections of important days results in a much richer memoir for the fireside years than "Becky bit Carla and called her a cow."

PEN PALS

Yuko lives in Japan and writes regularly to Harriet in Scotland. They have never met but have exchanged photos. They write about everyday stuff: hairstyles, hamsters, and Harry

"Focus should be to encourage and develop creativity in all children without the ultimate goal being to make all children inventors, but rather to develop a future generation of critical thinkers."
FARAQ MOUSA

Defining idea...

Why not put on an exhibition of words and pictures. Encourage your pre-teens to provide a commentary to photos, illustrations, and models (see IDEA 48, *Arty facts*).

Try another idea...

"A word is a bud attempting to be a twig. How can one not dream when writing? It is the pen which dreams. The blank page gives the right to dream."
GASTON BACHELARD, French scientist, philosopher, and literary theorist

Defining idea...

229

Potter. Harriet loves receiving beautifully folded letters with exotic looking stamps and postmarks. Yuko was worried about writing in English, but writing to Harriet has made learning easier and it doesn't feel like work. Email has made the world smaller, but pen pals make it magical.

A REAL BIND

After children have made up people and plots and committed them to paper, ask them to illustrate their work and make a book cover, title, and contents page for a professional finish. To produce a simple book, punch a pair of holes and tie a ribbon through them. Sophisticates can go to a local stationery shop for cheap binding.

DRAMA QUEENS

Drama queens and kings sometimes dislike writing because it seems like a quiet activity with limited opportunities for showing off. Suggest they write a play and produce it. If everyone dresses up for the first night, you'll get them on the *write* track.

How did it go?

Q **Tommy, who is eight, never got the hang of spelling. We know he's bright but his inability to spell is holding him back. His teacher just says that there are others much worse than he is. What can we do to help?**

A *It might be worth getting Tommy formally tested by a psychologist. He may have specific reading problems that he needs help with. You might also consider teaching him to type, which often improves spelling dramatically. Spell-checkers are not perfect but they do alert kids to words the computer doesn't recognize. Sooner or later, even the worst spellers improve.*

50

Dealing with death

Death, one of life's few certainties, may be an alien concept for pre-teens who've never been confronted by this loss. How can you help?

Children grieve as much as adults, but display grief differently. You can't and shouldn't stop children from feeling sad when someone dies, but you can learn how to help them with unfamiliar feelings and teach them to live with loss.

Helping children manage grief helps them understand and cope with this stressful and confusing time.

Children understand death differently at different ages:

- Two- to five-year-olds do not usually understand that death is permanent and irreversible.
- Six- to eight-year-olds know death is final but do not always realize it is inevitable.
- From nine years and up, children understand that death will happen to us all.

Here's an idea for you...

If death is expected, for example, if your father-in-law has terminal cancer or is very old, prepare children. Talk honestly about what is going to happen and allow them to say good-bye. They might want to start making their memory album.

Other factors affecting the intensity of grief are the relationship your child had with the deceased, the type of death, and reactions of family and friends. Pre-teens learn to grieve by observing adults.

COMMUNICATION

Try to be clear and honest, and be prepared to repeat bad news. Adjust explanations to the child's age. Sugar-coating using euphemisms like "Mommy has gone on a journey" or "Grandpa is asleep" is at best confusing and only demonstrates that you are incapable of conveying bad news in a digestible way. Although phrases like this may feel more comfortable to you, they increase the possibility of misunderstandings and could, for example, make kids frightened of going to sleep or cause them to wait for Grandpa to wake up. Encourage questions and reassure children that they are not responsible for the death. They may also need to be reassured that other members of the family and friends are well and not likely to die soon.

FUNERALS

Let children participate in funeral arrangements as much as they want to. Explain what will happen and consider taking them to the chapel or graveyard beforehand.

Defining idea...

"Life does not cease to be funny when people die any more than it ceases to be serious when people laugh."
GEORGE BERNARD SHAW

Allow them to see the body if they want to unless it is severely traumatized by the mode of death. You might worry that this will distress them unnecessarily, but this doesn't happen if they are told what to expect; for example, that the person's eyes will be closed and they will feel cold. We've seen children who felt angry and upset when they were not allowed to see the body and felt cheated out of a final good-bye. It helps if they can be involved in formal mourning rituals. Ask if they would like to choose a song, poem, or reading. Younger children may like to draw a picture to put in the coffin; older ones might want to write a letter.

MEMORIES

Cherishing special memories is an important part of grieving. Remembering helps children (and adults) internalize qualities of the dead person and move on. Many children like to make a memory box filled with things that help them remember like letters, photos, items of jewelery, the deceased's favorite book, or even recipes. Alternatively, your family could make a special album of letters, photographs, pressed funeral flowers, and everyone's favorite memory of the dead person. When grief is fresh, they might look in the box or at the album fairly often, but later they might just use it on anniversaries. Children may need practical ways to remember on the date of death, birthday, and other important days like Christmas, Thanksgiving, or Eid. Many don't know what to do when visiting the grave. Instead of flowers, they might like to take a drawing, handmade card, or a photocopy of a good report card. When a child or young person dies, setting up a school prize for a subject they excelled in can be a practical tribute. Why not plant a tree or shrub at the child's favorite park and have a plaque inscribed.

Try another idea...

Grief can be detrimental to children's self-esteem. If they feel bad about themselves, have trouble sleeping, or are falling behind at school, you might like to look at IDEA 35, *Highflyers*. Children can be comforted by having something special to look after and nurture, like a pet (see IDEA 28, *All creatures grate and smell*).

Defining idea...

"While grief is fresh, every attempt to divert it only irritates. You must wait till it be digested, and then amusement will dissipate the remains of it."
DR. SAMUEL JOHNSON

233

How did
it go?

Q   **My partner died last year. Sometimes my son wants to talk about his dad and remember him, but at other times he just seems fine and happy. I never know what to do or say, as I can't tell what mood he will be in.**

A   *Children can flit in and out of grief very quickly. It is normal for him to be very unhappy one minute and seem fine the next. We haven't found a reliable way of guessing how kids feel. Ask him what he wants.*

Q   **My mother is terminally ill. The children are very close to their grandmother and I don't want to upset them by telling them she is dying. Surely when they are little it is better to protect them from the truth, which would be very upsetting?**

A   *Don't underestimate your children's detective powers. Parents are often surprised at how many "adult secrets" children already know. Parental sadness, altered body language, and whispered conversations between adults are clues they pick up on. Uncertainty and not knowing is painful, too, and often harder for children to bear than a very sad truth.*

Q   **My daughter wants to read a poem at her friend's funeral, but I am worried she won't be up to it on the day.**

A   *Why not find out if it can be recorded in advance and played during the service? Recording it gives her the chance to get it just right and she can always read it live at the funeral if she feels able to. The friend's family may be very touched to have a tape to keep as a reminder of her thoughtfulness.*

51

After the affair

Breaking up may be hard to do, but living with that decision is even harder. We don't claim to have all the answers, but there are things here to soften the impact on your pre-teens.

Marriages may or may not be made in heaven. What is more certain is that when parents separate and go their different ways, everyone goes through hell. For the sake of the children, what can be salvaged from the wreckage?

COURTING DISASTER?

More and more marriages are ending in court. The implications for children and families are massive, usually leading to instability and emotional and fiscal uncertainty. The sweet singing from the same song sheet (see Idea 19) is suddenly replaced by disharmony and cacophony as everyone loses their place. Worried because your pre-teens are behind with schoolwork, or being aggressive and

Here's an idea for you...

Children in the throws of family breakdown need consistency more than ever. If you and your ex can agree for the sake of the children to apply family rules in both houses with equal sanctions for misdeeds, you'll both see less confusion, acting out, and manipulation. However angry and hurt you feel about your former partner, if you're able to continue singing from the same song sheet, the less likely your children are to blame themselves.

Defining idea...

"When I can no longer bear to think of the victims of broken homes, I begin to think of the victims of intact ones."
PETER DE VRIES, novelist, satirist, author of *Tunnel of Love*

defiant? Or your usually well-behaved pre-teens are in trouble, miserable, and think everything is their fault? Fallout from parental separation can be like this, but it won't last and there is a lot you can do to reduce it.

TELLING THE CHILDREN

Most parents who decide to separate worry about what to tell their children. We know a couple who explained divorce as "getting unmarried." Spare them stories about Dad's extramarital activities in the sauna with his secretary, but be up front so they don't have false hopes. "Sometimes relationships don't work and it's sad, but we'll all feel better again." Instead of "Your father's a bastard and I hate him," try "Daddy and I still like each other but not enough to want to live together anymore."

- Two- to five-year-olds find divorce or separation difficult to understand. They might fall back developmentally for a while, have problems with potty training or use babyish language. Tantrums, tears, and attention-seeking are common but short-lived reactions.

■ Six- to eight-year-olds are able to begin to understand what divorce or separation means. Many grieve deeply over family breakdown, pining for the parent that has left.

■ Nine- to twelve-year-olds are better able to understand what divorce or separation means. Many feel ashamed, resentful, or angry toward one or both parents.

SURVIVAL STRATEGIES: WHAT YOU CAN DO

1. Listen. Check out Idea 23, *Listen and learn.*

2. Make sure they know it's not their fault. Pre-teens can struggle to understand that you are separating from each other, not them.

3. Speak to their school. Teachers notice changes in concentration, friendships, and academic achievements, and if they know what is happening at home, they might be more empathetic and less punitive.

4. Sometimes it's tempting to overcompensate, showering pre-teens with presents. But giving presents is no substitute for actually telling children that you love them, however embarrassing this may be.

Defining idea...

"We all have troubles, great or small, and we all take them out on our children to some degree."
DR. BENJAMIN SPOCK, pediatrician and child-rearing guru

Try another idea...

Like the death of a parent or grandparent, parental separation causes grief. Why not look at making a memory book in IDEA 50, *Dealing with death*, as a way of acknowledging and celebrating the former home and family, recognizing what has been lost?

Defining idea...

"I don't feel caught in the middle. I hate them both equally."
NIGEL FULLERTON, eleven and a half years old

5. Whatever he or she's done to you, try not to criticize your ex in front of the children. Too often, we've seen kids caught in the crossfire between warring parents.

DIVORCE: A BEGINNING, NOT AN ENDING

It feels perverse to contemplate a positive side to separation. But just because divorce marks the end of a relationship, doesn't mean it can't represent a fresh start: New homes free of fighting parents and new members of the family could enhance rather than destroy the pre-teen years. Double allowance isn't bad either.

MOM'S "SPECIAL FRIEND"

Many parents are lucky enough to make new relationships. Nevertheless, introducing a new partner and his children to your kids is rarely easy. Honesty helps. Sidestep phrases such as "Mom's special friend," undermine pre-teens, who usually know more than we think. Giving kids guidance on how to address your new partner helps eliminate some of the inevitable awkwardness. Making the first meeting activity-based, and letting your pre-teen and partner spend time alone together after they've met a few times, helps them hit it off.

Q   **I'm really trying to give my children well-balanced meals and reinforce school with limited TV and structured homework time. When they go to their dad's, all they get is a diet of junk food and videos. He always thought I was too strict and now that we're not together, he refuses to budge. What can I do?**

How did it go?

A   *We hardly need tell you that different meals and regimes in different households are confusing and disruptive. Sometimes it helps "weekend" dads to get more involved in the responsible parts of parenting. Perhaps he'd like to attend a school parents' evening with you, and be more involved with the children's homework. Maybe he could also be encouraged to teach your children to cook (Idea 43, Little chef) and they all might be diverted away from takeout.*

Q   **Samantha, seven, is distressed on Monday mornings after being with my ex and his new wife for the weekend. Should I stop these visits?**

A   *While we can sympathize with your desire to terminate her visits, short-term gains will be replaced by longer-term problems. Parenting expert Dr. Sal Severe has described what he calls "Monday morning re-entry" syndrome. In a nutshell, this describes how children are just getting used to living with an occasional parent when it is time to go home again. Paradoxically, more rather than less contact and involvement with the non-custodial parent is recommended. Weekends are hardly long enough to bond.*

52

Something for the weekend

Dreading another frantic forty-eight hours? Want a happy weekend? Parents who plan can.

Create weekend traditions and rituals. It doesn't matter what you do—attend a religious service, have a special dinner every Friday night, go to a museum on Saturday afternoons—as long as there is some sense of routine and repetition connecting children to weekends past and future, creating a sense of belonging.

Pre-teens who learn to do things with family develop the art of negotiating and realize the importance of compromise.

We know it's the last thing you feel like doing, but drawing up a quick itinerary on Friday evening makes weekends a huge success. Weekends go wrong when there are clashing commitments: Jonny has to be at rugby, David at football, and Serena at

Here's an idea for you...

Visit a pick-your-own fruit farm. Strawberries, raspberries, or blueberries were made for little hands and if you're lucky you might live near blackberry bushes, which you can pick for free. Fruit picking teaches pre-teens how it grows and about different tastes. To increase educational opportunities further, help them weigh what they picked and make cakes, jams, or packed lunches with their produce. Some pre-teens think the real purpose of going fruit picking is to eat as much as they can before the farmer's wife notices. We agree.

tennis—all at 2 p.m.—Dad's playing golf and Mom has to get her hair cut. Nobody's got clean clothes. And there's a bus strike. Once you've written down what everyone has planned, you can compromise on what you could do together. When your family plans the weekend, include some unplanned time, too. Families who try to cram too much in, without any time for relaxing, run into problems, especially if homework is suddenly discovered. Making an itinerary will also jog your memory: Where are the theater tickets, who's babysitting tomorrow?

If there are things your pre-teens do every week, like going skating, set up a schedule between Mom and Dad, so neither of you feels dumped on. If your kids do an activity with friends, why not set up a circle? The Glyde family set up a swimming circle three years ago. Every Saturday morning, one set of parents from one of five families takes all the other families' pre-teens swimming. "We were fed up spending every Saturday morning in the shallow end, so decided to find other parents who felt the same. The kids' swimming has improved and their confidence has grown and every month or so when I take the swimming circle, I really enjoy the novelty factor and seeing how much they've improved" The Khans set up a Saturday morning film club with six families in their neighborhood. Every Saturday morning, all the pre-teens descend on one household to watch DVDs. All the other parents have a free morning to go shopping, go to the gym, or go back to bed for the morning with breakfast and papers.

We know lots of parents have had bad experiences taking pre-teens to museums, but we've found that it's often because kids were unprepared or families tried to cram too much into one visit. Museums are great for pre-teens as long as you start in the gift shop. Make it clear beforehand that you won't be buying any rulers or pencils, but that each child can chose three postcards. Find a quiet corner and read them the blurb on the back. Find out why they chose them. What do they like? Next, help each child find the exhibits or paintings on the postcards they've chosen. You might end up running around the museum like this, missing things you'll probably want to linger over. Instead, help them put their postcard exhibits in context. An alternative plan is to read about museum exhibits beforehand. Let your children choose a floor to explore. Attempting a whole museum at once tends to be disastrous. Leaving when everyone is up for more is far better than dragging them around "just one more gallery" to get your money's worth.

Try another idea…

Spending your whole weekend cleaning and tidying up after your pre-teens? Share chores during the week (see IDEA 26, It's not my turn) and everyone can have the weekend off.

Defining idea…

"Outings are so much more fun if we can savor them through the children's eyes."
LAWANA BLACKWELL, *The Courtship of the Vicar's Daughter*

WALK ON THE WILD SIDE

Like many parents, you've probably wondered how you can persuade your pre-teens to come for a long walk on the weekend. We've got a few tricks.

A poo trail is a top favorite with under-fives, but also works well with older pre-teens with a scientific mind and dirty sense of humor. Before you poo-poo the idea, remember that pre-schoolers in particular are fascinated by feces. While you walk, pre-teens are given special responsibility for finding out which animal's footsteps you are following in by identifying their poo. Horse dung, cow pats, rabbit droppings, pigeon splatters, and doggie doo bring out the best in pre-teens usually bored on a walk, and if you introduce a bit of competition—"Who'll be the next to spot a poo and tell everyone what it is?"—you'll be surprised how far those little legs can go.

If you're walking with a group of friends or family, divide pre-teens into teams for a treasure hunt. While everyone gets their coats and shoes on, write a list of things for teams to find on the walk. Include some easy ones to get them going, like a yellow leaf, daisy, or acorn; some things they'll have to root around for, like a snail, earwig, or worm; and some harder treasures to keep the game going, like a coin, barrette, and four-leaf clover.

If you've got time, make a copy of the list for each group, but if it's an impromptu walk, assign yourself referee and shout out an item from the list for everyone to look for. Once a team has found it, they get a point, and everyone moves on to the next item. If each team has their own list, the first team to find all the items wins.

Q   **I often end up trying to take my five-year-old son for a walk alone, but he soon gets bored and wants to go home. How can I keep him interested?**

Try
another
idea...

A   *If you're walking with just one pre-teen, give him a magnifying glass to explore leaves, insects, flowers, and his fingernails. Older pre-teens can be especially walk-resistant. If so, try a night walk. A walk around their school or other familiar place is particularly good fun when it's just snowed. Take a big flashlight and notice nighttime sounds and shapes.*

Where it's at...

52 Brilliant Ideas

UNLEASH YOUR CREATIVITY
978-0-399-53325-9

LIVE LONGER
978-0-399-53302-0

SECRETS OF WINE
978-0-399-53348-8

DETOX YOUR FINANCES
978-0-399-53301-3

CELLULITE SOLUTIONS
978-0-399-53326-6

RAISING A HEALTHY EATER
978-0-399-53339-6

PERIGEE ℗ An imprint of Penguin Group (USA)

one good idea can change your life

RAISING PRE-TEENS
978-0-399-53364-8

LAND YOUR DREAM JOB
978-0-399-53369-3

**BOOST YOUR
HEART HEALTH**
978-0-399-53376-1

DISCOVER YOUR ROOTS
978-0-399-53322-8

DEFEAT DEPRESSION
978-0-399-53373-0

SLEEP DEEP
978-0-399-53323-5

Available wherever books are sold or at penguin.com